LITTLE IRELAND

ASPECTS OF THE IRISH AND GREENHILL, SWANSEA

LITTLE IRELAND

ASPECTS OF THE IRISH AND GREENHILL, SWANSEA

R. T. Price

City of Swansea
1992

The publication of this book by Swansea City Council does not necessarily imply the Council's official approbation of the opinions expressed herein.

First published 1992 by Swansea City Council.
Obtainable from the City Archives Office, Central Services Department, Guildhall, Swansea, SA1 4PE.

City Archives Publications: Studies in Swansea's History, no. 1.

ISBN 0 946001 21 9

General Editor:
J.R. Alban, B.A., Ph.D., D.A.A., City Archivist.

Contents

List of Maps, Illustrations And Photographs

List of Abbreviations

CLS - *Catholic Life in Swansea*
ECMW - *Early Christian Monuments of Wales*
GCH - *Glamorgan County History*
IFN - *Irish Family Names*
ILN - *The Illustrated London News*
ISPAH - *The Irish Sea Province in Archaeology and History*
JCHAS - *Journal of the Cork Historical and Archaeological Society*
JRSAI - *Journal of the Royal Society of Antiquarians of Ireland*
SPM - *Saint Peter's Magazine*
SRSI - *Special Report on Surnames in Ireland*
SW - *Sundays in Wales*
THSC - *Transactions of the Honourable Society of Cymmrodorion*
UCS - University College of Swansea, Library

General Editor's Preface

Since its appearance in 1989, Roger Price's thesis on 'The Origin of the Irish in Greenhill' has been consulted by many researchers, and has been frequently referred to in scholarly studies. The thesis was not a chronological account of Irish settlement and the development of the suburb of Greenhill; nor was it a detailed examination of the social scene in that part of industrial Swansea. Rather, it sought to investigate the links between Ireland and South Wales, and particularly with Swansea, and to consider the antecedents of those Irish folk who came to a town which, by the early years of the nineteenth century, was developing as a major industrial and commercial centre, not just in British terms, but in the sphere of the wider world. However, the thesis also shed light on events in Greenhill during the early years of Irish settlement there, up to the 1860s, by investigating primary sources such as the Health Reports, newspapers, together with the evidence of the censuses.

In one sense, the thesis was a foundation upon which further studies could be built, and, thus, it has been regarded as a source of inspiration. However, the fact that only one copy exists, and that in an academic library, means that it has not had the general currency which it deserves. The establishment of the 'Studies in Swansea's History' series has at last provided a welcome opportunity to make this work available to a wider, general audience. Furthermore, while studies are now appearing on Irish communities in other parts of Wales, little, as yet, has appeared on the Swansea Irish, so that the publication of Mr Price's work in this series will hopefully serve as a starting point for further study. Largely following the approach of the original thesis, the work is full of lively anecdotes, and,moreover, the comprehensive excerpts from the census enumerators' returns between 1841 and 1861 will be a valuable reference source for family historians as well as for those persons whose interest in the history of Swansea is more general.

'Studies in Swansea's History', of which this is the first volume, is intended to be series of monographs on specific aspects of the history of Swansea and Gower, written by local historians and based upon original research. The series is published by Swansea City Council's City Archives Office, and titles will be appearing regularly. It is hoped that, over the years, the series will develop into a solid corpus of local historical reference, of interest to both scholar and public alike.

J.R. Alban

Acknowledgements

I wish to acknowledge the following persons by name for their help and encouragement in the preparation of this study: Dr John Alban, Father Leo Bonsall, Ken Brooks, Jan Greengo, Mike Hannen, Paul O'Leary, Ursula Masson, Betty Nelmes, Bill Pring, William Quigley, R.O. Roberts, and also the staff of Swansea Central Reference Library and my colleagues in University College Swansea Library. Thanks are also due to the University of Wales Press and the National Museum of Wales for permission to reproduce the illustration at Plate 3. Last, but not least, I wish to thank my wife, Ruth.

Introduction

There are many reasons why I chose to write the thesis on which this book is based. Firstly, my great-grandfather, John Patrick Mallon, of County Tyrone, was one of the nineteenth-century Irish immigrants into the Swansea area. This fact, coupled with my personal interest in the links between the Celtic peoples made the subject attractive to me. Secondly, I believe that the substantial influx of Irish into Swansea during the nineteenth century, and the significant contribution which they have made to the city, has, to a great extent, been overlooked.

There have already been studies on the Irish communities of Cardiff and Merthyr Tydfil. J.V. Hickey's M.A. thesis on 'The Origin and Growth of the Irish Community in Cardiff' appeared in 1959, while in 1975 Ursula Masson wrote an M.A. thesis, 'The Development of the Irish and Roman Catholic Communities of Merthyr Tydfil and Dowlais, in the Nineteenth Century'. Many parts of the Principality were covered in Paul O'Leary's 'Immigration and Integration: a Study of the Irish inWales, 1798-1922' (Ph.D. thesis, University of Wales, 1989). Nevertheless, there remains no study specifically dealing with the Swansea Irish, and I felt that I would like to redress the balance in some small way.

I also felt that I had to write about the early links between Wales and Ireland, to put nineteenth-century Irish immigration into its wider context. The narrative introductory section, is followed by a section devoted to the growth of the Roman Catholic Church in Swansea. Although this does not deal exclusively with the Irish themselves, the fortunes of the Irish and their Roman Catholic religion are inextricably linked. For Chapter I, secondary sources were plentiful, but not so for Chapter II. The most useful information was to be found in the well researched articles by J.M.C. Cronin in *Saint Peter's Magazine*, written during the 1920s.

Chapter III is based exclusively on the Health Reports of the 1840s and 1850s. There was a wealth of material in the local newspapers of the 1840s and 1850s, but owing to availability of space, I have limited myself to covering certain topics, such as the latent tensions between Welsh and Irish workers during the first half of the nineteenth century. The sympathy of newspaper editorials towards the plight of the Irish during the famine starkly contrasts with their attitude towards the Irish poor on their own doorstep. Chapter IV contains excerpts from a series of articles about the living conditions in Greenhill in 1853, which corroborate the descriptions contained in the Health Reports of the previous chapter. The final chapter refers to data collected and collated from the Census Enumerators' Returns for Swansea of 1841, 1851 and 1861.

I conclude with a discussion of the Irish Ballad 'The Holy Ground', and its Swansea origin, as a means to bring this study full-circle, to indicate the two-way process of cultural borrowings, and as yet more evidence of the maritime links between the port of Swansea and Cork Harbour. So the book ends where it began, along the established sea routes between South Wales and southern Ireland.

R. T. Price

CHAPTER ONE

Historical Relations Between South Wales and Southern Ireland, *c.* 400 - *c.* 1800

Both Wales and Ireland are centrally situated on what has been termed the 'Western Seaways', which stretch from Caithness to Galicia. Several eminent twentieth-century geographers, such as H.J. Mackinder and E.G. Bowen, have emphasised the importance of the western seaways in linking the peoples of Celtic culture through the ages. Mackinder defined the British Seas as consisting of two portions: the narrow seas separating the lowland zone of England from the continent of Europe, and the seas lying to the west and north of highland Britain which have later become known as the Western Seas. The Western Seas he sub-divided into three sections. That section which concerns us here he called 'the Marine Antechamber of Britain' or the 'Channel Entries' (see Map 1). This is the 'Celtic Sea' of our contemporary age, i.e., the seas lying between Brittany, Cornwall, south-west Wales and southern Ireland[1]. The concept of an Irish Sea Culture Province has also been given prominence in more recent years because archaeological finds of different periods show a definite cultural link along these ancient lines of communication, and this is supported by interpretation of the cartographical representation of archaeological material in the lands bordering the Western Seas[2].

With the collapse of Roman rule in Britain towards the end of the fourth century AD, and the subsequent invasion of the lowland zone of Britain by the Anglo-Saxons, the western sea-routes once again became more active. This sub-Roman or 'Dark Age' period was a formative period in the history of the British Isles. It was the age of folk migrations, not only of the Germanic invaders into what would become England, but also of the 'British' colonisation of Armorica, otherwise known as Brittany, and also the settlement of Argyll by the *Scotti* of Ulster, who gave their name and Gaelic culture to Scotland.

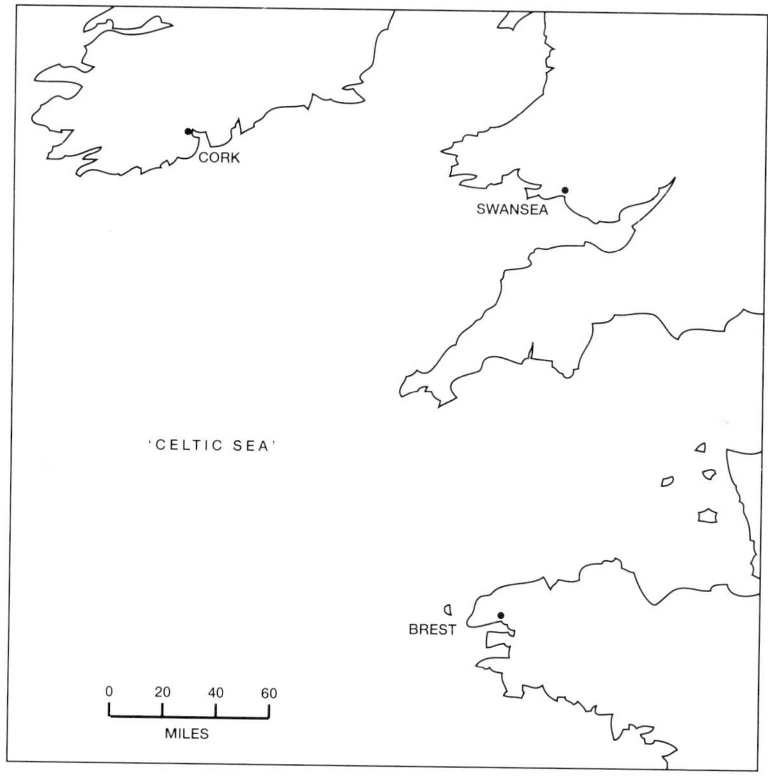

Map 1: The Marine Antechamber of Britain.

There was another Irish colonisation of western Britain, which, although having less enduring qualities than that further north, was nevertheless equally significant in displaying the close ties which exist between the Celtic peoples. That was the settlement of the Déisi and Uí Liatháin in parts of south-west Wales. They came originally from the southern seaboard of Ireland, between Cork and Waterford (see Maps 4 and 5). This movement can fairly reliably be assigned to the late fourth and early fifth centuries AD.

Map 2: Distribution of Ogham inscribed stones in the British Isles.

All the evidence shows that it was the extreme south-west of Wales which experienced the heaviest settlement of Irish people. The importance of the Dyfed settlement lies in the fact that for perhaps 400 years there was an Irish kingdom in Wales. The earthwork known as

Plates 1 and 2: Clawdd Mawr, Dyfed

Clawdd Mawr, situated on the watershed between the Tywi and Teifi river systems marks the eastern border of this Irish kingdom (see Plates 1 and 2). To the east of Clawdd Mawr lay the kingdom of Ystrad Tywi. To the east of Ystrad Tywi was the kingdom of Brycheiniog, which also had a strong Irish presence, epitomised by its semi-mythical king, Brychan (Irish. *Broccan*), the reputed Irish founder of the dynasty. Ystrad Tywi, situated between these two Irish or Irish influenced kingdoms, was a sort of Brythonic wedge which stretched down as far as the Gower peninsula. But according to the Welsh chronicler, Nennius and the Irish chronicler, Cormac there was a movement of the Irish tribe called the Uí Liatháin into Cydweli and Gower, although some authorities are doubtful about this[3].However, there is a strong likelihood that the Irish did settle in the coastal belt between Dyfed and Morgannwg. Indications of this are supplied by place-names, early Christian monuments and memorial stones. The Welsh word *cnwc* (hillock) is known to be a borrowing from the Irish word *cnoc* (hill/hillock); the native Welsh name being *cnwch*. The *cnwc* names in Wales are most in evidence in the extreme south-west of Wales, but there are two such names in West Glamorgan - Cnwc Coch at Llansamlet, Swansea, and Cae Cnwc near Aberafan. The river name Clydach with its *-ach* termination also shows Goidelic influence, the mountain called Drumau, near Neath may also contain the Irish Gaelic word for ridge, *drum*, and there are many other examples. Place-names can give some clues to be used in evidence where there is a shortage of historical facts, but we are on surer ground when it comes to the evidence furnished by the Ogham memorial stones.

These Ogham memorial stones represent the archaeological evidence for the settlement of the Déisi and the Uí Liatháin, being linked philologically and geographically with similar memorial stones that occur in large numbers in southern Ireland. This script has been shown to have developed in Ireland (possibly Munster, where the greatest concentration of Ogham inscriptions are to be found), sometime in the fourth century AD. From Ireland it spread to western Britain in the fifth century. In Britain, Ogham stones are most numerous in South Wales (see Maps 2 and 3). It is significant that of the known inscriptions about five-sixths have been found in Ireland, whilst of these Irish inscriptions, about five-sixths occur in the counties of Kerry, Cork and Waterford. About forty Ogham inscriptions have come to light in Wales, of which fifteen are in Pembrokeshire. Glamorganshire has four, two within the Swansea region at Loughor and Kenfig (see Figs. 1 and 2).

In addition to the place-name evidence and the Ogham inscribed stones, there are other carved stones in our region which exhibit definite Irish influence (See Plate 3). The so-called 'Leper Stone' at Llanrhidian has a pair of human figures with the usual 'Celtic' oval faces.

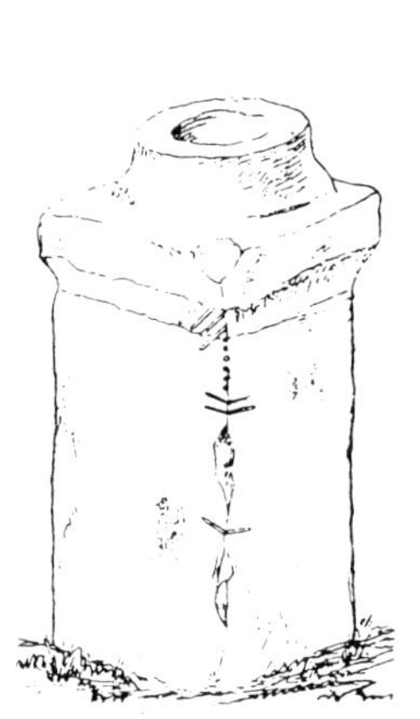

Figure 1

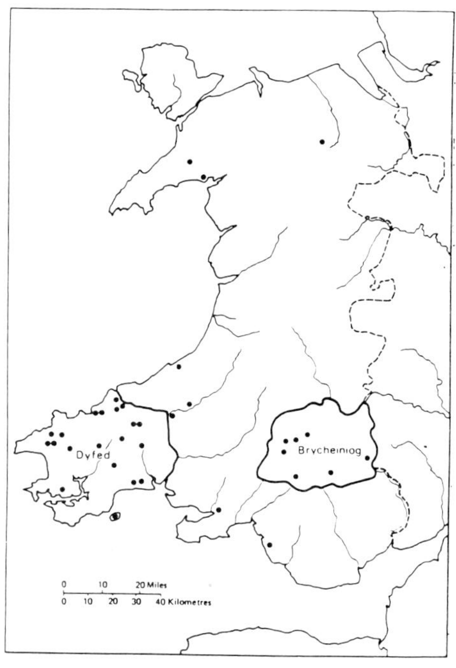

Map 3: The distribution of stones Irish Ogham inscriptions in Wales.

Figure 1: Roman altar with Ogham inscription, Loughor.

Figure 2: Ogham Stone, Kenfig.

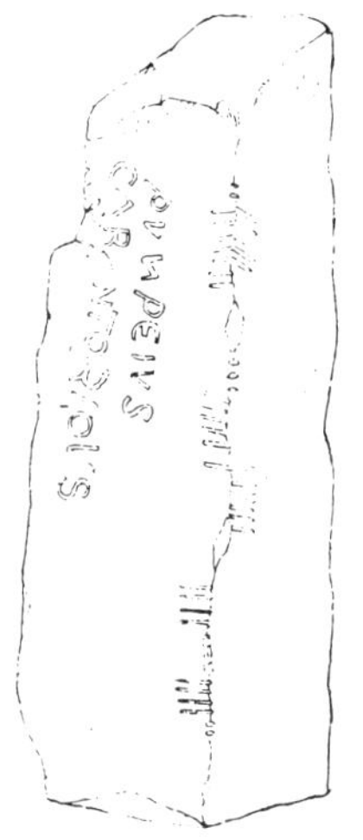

Figure 2

Plate 3: Early Christian Monuments from West Glamorgan
(University of Wales Press/National Museum of Wales).

The stone at Gelli Onnen, near Pontardawe also shows Irish features. Its figure appears to be wearing a cape of a similar style to the illustration of St Matthew in the Book of Durrow[4]. The third monument comes from Cefn Hirfynydd. This period has been termed the 'Age of the Celtic Saints' and there was a great deal of contact between the Irish and Welsh churches. Apart from the obvious references to St David being half Irish and St Patrick being a Briton, there were other examples of close contact.

St Cadog, we are told, wished to build an oratory in Neath and engaged twelve workmen for the purpose:

> Wherefore it happened that a certain Irishman named Liuguri (probably

Laogaire), a stranger but a skilful architect, being forced by poverty, came to him with his children and family.[5]

If this story is true, it would make him one of the earliest Irish construction workers in Wales!

The Age of the Saints which was the 'Golden Age' of Ireland was brought to an end by the incursions of the Vikings, who made permanent settlements on the Irish coast, most notably in Dublin, Cork,Wexford, Waterford, and Limerick. It was these Norse, or Norwegian Vikings who raided and settled in the highland zone of northern and western Britain, and not the Danes whose activities were mainly concentrated on the lowland zone of eastern England. In Ireland, Norse kingdoms were set up after the last decade of the eighth century. It was inevitable that Wales, from its geographical position in the centre of the zone of Viking activities, should also feel the impact of the great Scandinavian invasions in the west. The coastline of parts of Wales was fully exposed to invasions from the Norse colonies of Ireland. It is arguable that Wales, like Ireland and western Britain, was mostly in contact with the Norwegian branch of Scandinavian raiders, particularly since most of the early raids originated from the Norse settlements in Ireland, especially that of the 'Ostmen' of Dublin.

Relations through Christianity and trade between Ireland and Wales had been established centuries prior to the Scandinavian period, so that the closer and more frequent relations of the ninth, tenth, eleventh, and twelfth centuries were really a national development. The early raids from Ireland soon changed in the first half of the eleventh century into Norse-Welsh amicable alliances against a common foe, the Anglo-Saxons of England. 'Armes Prydein' (the 'Omen of Britain'), was a poem composed in the form of a prophecy of an ideal future state. It was predicted by a patriotic bard that the day would come when Cadwaladr and Cynan would return to deliver the Welsh from their hated Saxon or *Allmyn*, 'foreign' oppressors, and peace reign over the land. To bring about the desired end a great league, consisting of the Ostmen of Dublin, the Irish (or Norse-Irish) of Ireland, Mon (the Isle of Man) and Scotland, and also the men of Cornwall and Strathclyde,would join the Welsh:

Achymot Kymry a gwyr Dulyn
Gwydyl Iwerdon Mon a Phrydyn
Cornyw a Chludwys eu kynwys genhyn
Atporyon uyd Brython pan dyorfyn
Pell dygoganher amser dybydyn . . .

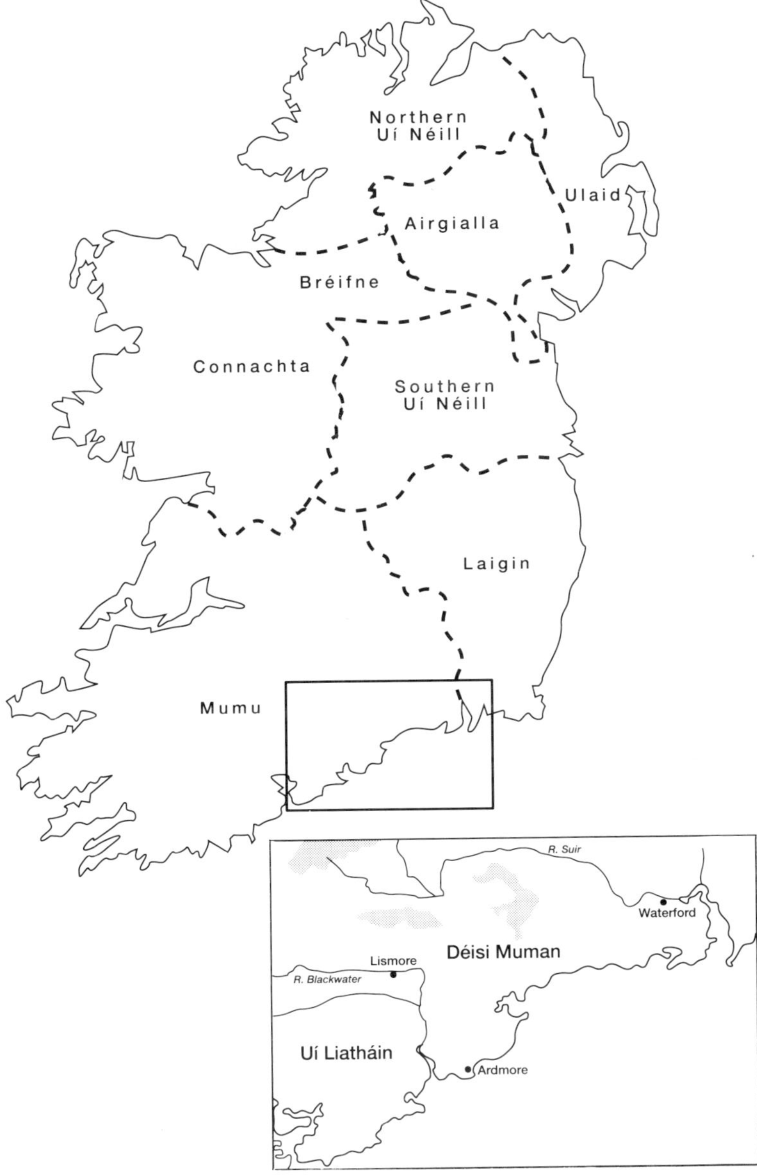

Maps 4 and 5: Coast of Munster where the Déisi and the Liatháin were settled.

The following stanza alluded even more specifically to Irish aid:

> Gwyr gwychyr gwallt hiryon ergyr dofyd o dihol Saesson o Iwerdon dybyd.
> (Valiant men with long hair and expert warriors shall come from Ireland to banish the Saxons.)

This poem was written sometime between 836 and 1066. Owing to the fact that Dublin was founded by the Vikings in 836, and the Saxons were conquered by the Normans in 1066, Sir Ifor Williams, an authority on the poem, gives the date as *c*. 930[6].

The seaport towns of Ireland - Dublin, Limerick, Waterford, Cork and Wexford - owe their origin and growth to the Norsemen who settled there in the ninth and tenth centuries, and there are good reasons to believe that from their well-established towns in Ireland the Norsemen developed a flourishing trade with South Wales and the Bristol Channel. They were undoubtedly responsible for the development of some of the chief seaport towns of South Wales, such as the Norse-named Swansea, or *Sweinsey*. When it is remembered how intimate was the political connection between Norse Ireland and Wales from the ninth century to the middle of the twelfth century and how persistently the Viking raiders harried the Welsh coast, it was almost inevitable that Norse traders should seek new homes for the expansion of their commerce along the coast of South Wales, at suitable harbours such as Swansea. As early as the twelfth century, there are positive links between Swansea and Ireland. Godafridus and Ricardus filius Segeri, both hailing from *Sweinesea*, are mentioned in the Dublin roll of names[7].

After 980, Norse mercenaries from Ireland were frequently hired by Welsh princes, both against the English and against native Welsh antagonists. The Norse kingdoms of Ireland were the asylums of Welsh refugees. The intimate connection between Wales and the Norsemen of Ireland at the beginning of the eleventh century is illustrated by the presence of Welsh auxiliaries at the eventful battle of Clontarf, in 1014, but it is almost certain that these were Norsemen who had settled in the Welsh towns and not native Welsh. The Scandinavians who settled in Ireland continued to play an important part in Welsh political events until the English conquest of Ireland, with which came the termination of all relations between the Welsh and the Norsemen.

The approaches through the Irish Sea and the southern channel, from England, Wales and north-western France, led directly into the desirable regions of Ireland. In historical times the Vikings had established their permanent settlements mainly, south-east of a line from Dublin to Limerick, while the Anglo-Normans spread their conquest over the whole of the lowland coastal area, 'the Pale' scarcely penetrating far into the interior[8]. Giraldus Cambrensis tells us that Robert Fitzstephen who landed in Ireland in 1169, was accompanied by 300 archers on foot, 'the flower of the youth of Wales'. Robert de Barri, brother of Gerald, was among the little band of Norman knights who affected the first landing at Bannow Bay, Co. Wexford on 1 May, 1169. He took a prominent part in the assault on Wexford town shortly afterwards, and in the taking of Limerick in the following year. After the Norman invasion in 1169 Robert Fitzstephen and Maurice Fitzgerald, some of the adventurers who accompanied the expedition of Richard Fitzgilbert de Clare, better known as 'Strongbow', settled in lands assigned to them in the south-east corner of Wexford, in a district now known as the baronies of Forth and Bargy. There were infantrymen who were Normans, Flemings, Welsh and English among them. It is a simple historical fact that their descendants still inhabit the same corner of Wexford, a triangle of land between Wexford town, Bannow Bay and Carnsore Point, where numerous names such as Pate, Codd, Strafford, Devereux, Lambert, Rossiter and Browne still predominate[9].

The early settlers, within a century of 1169, seem to have settled down to the kind of life they knew in Pembrokeshire and Glamorganshire. Down to the middle of the last century, many of their ancient, social and domestic manners and customs, and a dialect of English which, during its decline, they began to call Yola, their word for old, continued to survive.

The following is the Lord's Prayer from Forth, collected at the end of the last century:

> Oure vaader fho yarth ing heaveene, ee-hallowet bee t'naame.
> Thee kingdim coome, thee weel be ee-doane, as ing heaveene,
> zo eake an earthe, yee ouze todeie oure deilye breed, an varyee ouze
> our dettes, as wough varyee our dettores; an leed ouze nat in to varsaakeen, mot
> varlouse ouze vrom evil. Vur theen are ee kingdome an ee creft an ee lordly
> heed, ing ayeheede, amein[10].

Further west in County Cork the twelfth-century Cambro-Norman invasion brought warfare and widespread disruption to most parts of the county, but the conquest was never completed. By the sixteenth century, the position was that, if one drew a line roughly from Kinsale northwards through Mallow, almost all the lands to the west of that were occupied by families of Gaelic descent.

Eastwards, lords of Norman origin ruled - principally, the Barrys, Roches, Condons and Fitzgeralds (see Map 6). The O'Driscolls, O'Mahonys and O'Sullivans are still most numerous on the western peninsulas. About the year 1180 Philip de Barri received from his uncle Robert Fitzstephen (the grantee of the eastern portion of the 'Kingdom of Cork') a sub-infeudation of three cantreds - Olethan, Muskery-Donegan and Killyde. Olethan, the former Uí Liatháin tribeland, is now known as Barrymore. Castle Lyons was built sometime in the first half of the thirteenth century, being known as *Castrum Olethan* or Caislean O'Liatháin - the castle of Uí Liatháin[11]. (The tribal lands of the Déisi in County Waterford are known today as the Decies). The de Barri family were originally settled in Barry, near neighbours of the Cogan and Canton families. The small parish of Cogan, between Penarth and Cardiff, gave its name to this Cambro-Norman family which rose to great eminence in Ireland in the thirteenth century, that of the de Cogan family. The de Condons' name first appeared in Ireland as 'de Caunteton', 'de Caunton', etc., that is of Caunteton or Caunton, the Canton area of Cardiff[12]. Pembrokeshire families were also prominent. The de Nagle or Nangle family originated in Angle in South Pembrokeshire. Jocelyn de Angulo was one of the warriors who served Hugh de Lacy, the first Norman Lord of Meath. The Roche family also came from Pembrokeshire where Roch castle remains to this day, between Haverfordwest and St David's[13].

Irish-Welsh family ties continued from the medieval period to the modern age. Historically, western Britain was usually at least as close in culture and society to Ireland as to the prosperous south-east of England. These relationships have been studied for the medieval and earlier periods, but links continued in much later ages, at least until British roads improved sufficiently to draw the west into a metropolitan ambit, perhaps after 1780[14].

The new phase in the relations between Wales and Ireland may be said to open with the early years of Elizabeth, when the two countries were given strategic unity by the appointment of Sir Henry Sidney to the less congenial Lord Deputyship of Ireland while he still remained

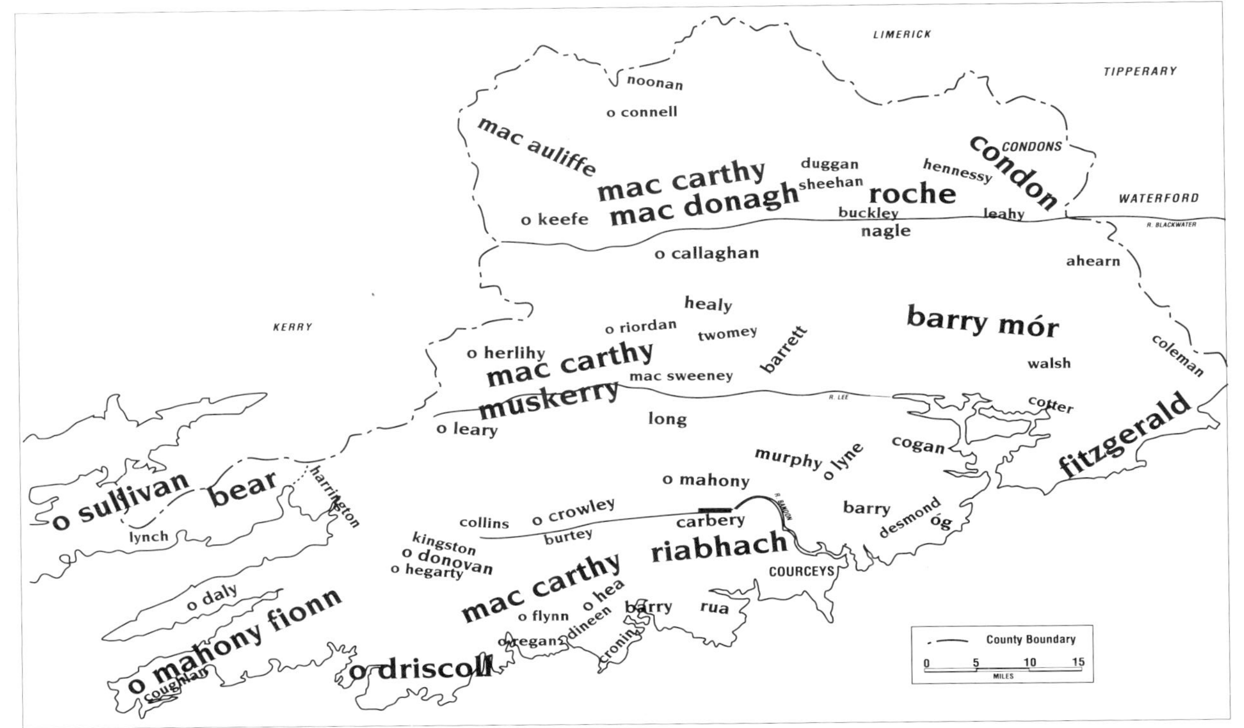

Map 6: Location of families in County Cork.

President of Wales. More significant still is the Irish rule of his successor Sir John Perrot. It was during Perrot's deputyship that the plantation of Munster drew closer bonds between Wales and the dominant minority in Ireland. Outstanding among the Munster 'undertakers' was Sir William Herbert of St Juliens, great grandson of the first Earl of Pembroke. He took out substantial allotments of forfeited land in Munster and went to live at Castleisland in Co. Kerry.

As well as family ties, trade formed another important link. During the Stuart period in the seventeenth century. Ireland was taking some sixty per cent of the small volume of exports that went overseas from Wales, such as coal from the South Wales ports of Swansea, Neath, and Llanelli. Welsh trade was fairly linked to the south and west. As well as the 'metropolitan' area of Bristol, other main areas of contact were south-west England, southern Ireland and western France. The Welsh Port Books have copious references to Bordeaux, Cork or Bridgewater, but virually none to the cities of northern or eastern England. Ireland was vital to Welsh trade, of coal especially, and particularly from the 1620s. The chief ports for this trade included Wicklow, Youghal and Waterford on the western side, and Milford Haven, Llanelli, Neath and Swansea on the eastern. Industrial growth in west Glamorgan from about 1700 led to an intensified search for raw materials, and existing family links helped. Copper was mined in the Wicklow mountains as well as in Cornwall and Anglesey. In 1728, Theobald Mathew of Thurles (from an old Glamorgan line) sent a consignment of copper to Swansea, and this trade continued for decades afterwards[15].

Sea communications across St George's Channel were well known, and a typical voyage is recorded in John Wesley's journal for August 1758, when he sailed from Queenstown (Cobh) to Penclawdd in Gower[16]. There would certainly have been many merchants and sailors well acquainted with both areas, and there had long been migration both ways across the channel, so that Swansea had inhabitants named Donnell or Cavanagh long before the great migrations from Ireland began in the 1780s. A Swansea Borough Ordnance for 15 December 1584, contains a reference to two Irishmen, namely William Tege and Daniell John, who were allowed to become burgesses of the town of Swansea[17]. A burgess by the name of Owen Donnell is named in the Swansea Common Hall Book on 8 December 1635[18]. At least from the sixteenth century there had been a strong Irish element in areas of south-west Wales. Names like Wogan and Stackpole were common both in Pembrokeshire and in parts of Ireland, but in few other places in the British Isles.

Personal contacts also arose through the military careers of Welsh squires, who served in Ireland. The Gower Roundhead, Henry Bowen, set up a new and long-enduring gentry family at Bowen's Court, between Mallow and Mitchelstown in County Cork. He was widely connected with the gentry of west Glamorgan. One of the most remarkable relationships may be traced between two very powerful lines,the Aubreys of Glamorgan and the Jephsons of Mallow, County Cork, who formed three marriage alliances in as many generations. Swansea became the destination of Protestant refugees, including Hugh Gore, bishop of Lismore and Waterford and, also, no doubt, for later political refugees, such as those who took part in the 1798 rebellion.

From the late eighteenth century onwards, it was the poorer class of Irish who were to dwell most heavily on the minds of the local establishment in South Wales. Glamorgan Quarter Sessions would long be concerned with the problem of isolated groups of Irish vagrants landing on the Welsh coast, and having to be despatched home. In July 1756, for example, a provision was made for the conveyance of Irish vagrants back to Ireland, listing the scale of allowances payable to parish constables who accompanied them to the nearest seaport, and to shipmasters who conveyed them across the Irish Sea[19].

Poverty and unemployment were widespread in Ireland in the eighteenth century, so that large numbers of Irish vagrants came into Glamorgan through ports such as Swansea. In Irish law there was no such thing as a place of settlement, so that Irish vagrants were sent back to Ireland under the Vagrancy Acts. A Justices' order of 1759 shows what happenend to a poor Irishwoman arrested as a vagrant in Swansea:

> Whereas Margaret Carty a rogue and vagabond was apprehended in the Town of Swansea in the said County, and upon her Examination taken in writing the Tenth day of June last before me one of his Majestys Justices of the Peace in and for the said County, did upon her oath, swear that the place of her legal settlement was in the City of Cork in the Kingdom of Ireland - and thereupon Benjamin Rees one of the Constables of the Town of Swansea aforesaid was ordered by warrant under my hand and seal to convey the said vagrant to the Mumbles in the said County and there to deliver her to Phillip Jeffreys master of the ship called the Prince of Orange then lying there and bound to the said City of Cork . . .[20]

This chapter has endeavoured to show the close connections between South Wales and southern Ireland over a period of more than a millenium, from the 'Golden Age' of Ireland to a period of poverty and starvation for the mass of the Irish people in the late eighteenth and early nineteenth centuries. The geographical proximity of the two countries, with their well-established sea-links, and also the shared Celtic culture, ensured continued intercourse between the two peoples. It is clear that in the nineteenth century, as in the days of the Celtic saints, the Irish Sea was to remain a pathway, rather than a moat.

However, economic and social events of the late eighteenth and early nineteenth centuries led to an intensifying of the links between Ireland and Swansea, and these culminated in the substantial influx of Irish into the town during the nineteenth century, and especially in the 1840s. Indeed, the potato famines of the latter decade have been seen as an important immediate cause for this migration, but there were also longer-term factors which drove Irish people to seek new lives elsewhere. The growing industrial centre of Swansea, by the same token, offered many opportunities to newcomers, and its proximity to the ports of southern Ireland increased its attraction to Irish emigrants.

During the eighteenth century ownership of land was the basis of wealth, social position and political power in Ireland, so in order for the Protestant minority to secure an 'ascendancy' over the Roman Catholic majority the Dublin parliament (which was subordinate to the parliament at Westminster) enacted the Penal Code or 'laws against popery'. In 1709 an act was passed which forbade Catholics to buy land or to take leases for longer than thirty-one years. By 1778 scarcely five per cent of the land of Ireland was left in the hands of the native Catholic Irish.

Another factor which accounts for the destitution of so many of the Irish was the rapid rise in population during the second half of the century, from about two and a half million in 1767 to over four million by 1781. This population explosion continued into the next century: over six million in 1821 to over eight million in 1841.It has been estimated that in 1841 about two-thirds of this huge population depended on the land for a living. The most insecure class were the labourers who rented plots of land for a cash rent and hence were obliged to find adequate wage-paid employment if they were to survive. All of these labourers were in a perilous economic situation in a labour market that was increasingly over supplied, therefore increasing numbers left Ireland to seek seasonal employment in Britain. The Great Famine from 1845 to 1850 was caused by the potato blight which destroyed the potato crops, the sole food of about one-third of the Irish and a crucial component in the diet of a considerably larger number. The effects were starvation, death or mass emigration.

Ireland had certain limitations on its economic potential owing to its lack of mineral resources, particularly coal. This is in stark contrast to South Wales, which had abundant supplies of coal, iron ore and other minerals and resources needed for industrial development. Swansea was the largest town in Wales at the beginning of the nineteenth century, and was expanding rapidly with the growth of industry and other commercial activity. As a sea-port with long-standing links with southern Ireland it attracted many Irish immigrants. Ironically, it was these Irish, fleeing from their native land, owing to the circumstances to which they had been subjected, that brought with them their Roman Catholic faith, and it was they, in great measure, who accounted for the revival of the Roman Catholic Church in Swansea, which will be discussed in the next chapter.

NOTES

1. H.J. Mackinder, *Britain and the British Seas* (Oxford, 1930), pp.19, 20.
2. E.G. Bowen, 'The Irish Sea in the Age of the Saints' in *Studia Celtica*, iv (1969), p.56.
3. L. Alcock, 'Was there an Irish Sea Culture-Province in the Dark Ages?' in *ISPAH*, ed. D. Moore, p.56; and also S.H. Cousens, 'Settlement before the Norman Conquest', in *Swansea and its Region*, ed. W.G.V. Balchin (Swansea, 1971), p.141.
4. V.E. Nash-Williams, *The Early Christian Monuments of Wales* (Cardiff, 1950), p.161.
5. K. Meyer, 'Early Relations between Gael and Brython', in *THSC* (1895-6), p.80.
6. I. Williams, *Armes Prydein*, xvii.
7. B.G. Charles, *Old Norse Relations with Wales* (Cardiff, 1934), pp.158-60: 'from the Historical and Municipal Documents of Ireland'.
8. C. O'Danachair, 'Irish Vernacular Architecture in Relation to the Irish Sea', in *ISPAH*, p.98.

9. D. O'Muirithe, 'The Anglo-Normans and their English Dialect of South-East Wexford', in *The English Language in Ireland*, ed. D. O'Muirithe (Dublin, 1977), p.77.
10. ibid., p.40.
11. D. O'Murchadha, *Family Names in County Cork* (Dun Laoghaire, 1985), p.23.
12. ibid., pp.77, 95.
13. ibid., p.256.
14. P. Jenkins, 'Connections between the Landed Communities of Munster and South Wales, *c*. 1660-1780', in *JCHAS*, xl (1985), p.95.
15. ibid., p.95.
16. ibid., p.95.
17. UCS, (1st) Swansea Borough Ordnance, no. 21, p.42.
18. UCS, (1st) Common Hall Book, no. 131, p.259.
19. Glamorgan Quarter Sessions M. vol. 2, pp.154, 155.
20. R.K.J. Grant, *On the Parish* (Cardiff, 1985), p.53.

Chapter Two

The Growth of the Roman Catholic Church in Swansea, 1808 - 1888

The Roman Catholic Church in Wales, as elsewhere in Britain, was at its weakest at the end of the eighteenth century. The depletion in the number of Welsh Catholics by this period left them concentrated geographically in the Welsh border counties, particularly in Flintshire and north-west Monmouthshire. In South Wales there had been small groups of Catholics (termed Papists or Recusants, depending on the point of view) in the principal towns, but not in such numbers sufficient to support a priest or a chapel. Brecon was one town where the old Catholic faith had never died out. There was always a permanent, but small, congregation of Catholics, possessing a place for mass in the Watergate, which was maintained by a priest, but nothing similar was to be found elsewhere in South Wales. The Franciscans, who were at Abergavenny, also served the town of Brecon, and sent out a priest four or five times a year.

In the eighteenth century, the whole of Wales was included in what the Roman Catholic Church called the Western District, or jurisdiction, which also embraced several English counties. In October 1773, Mgr. Charles Walmesley, Vicar Apostolic of this Western District, reported to Rome that there were only 750 Catholics in the whole of Wales. At the end of the eighteenth century the scattered remnants of the Roman Catholic community in South Wales were served by priests from Bristol. In 1814 Father Robert Plowden of Bristol, a Jesuit who was responsible for the South Wales Mission, wrote:

> I could never make the journey's required every year, whilst I served that mission, without being constantly out of pocket. The original allowance was (less property tax) £22 5s 1d. and the Welsh Mission to be served for this sum, was the whole course of South Wales, wherever there were Catholics, from Cardiff to Milford Haven inclusively . . .[1]

According to the census of 1801, Swansea had a population of 6,099, while Cardiff had 1,870. Thus Swansea was by far the most important town in the county of Glamorgan at this time. As a seaport it had constant intercourse with Bristol, Cornwall and Devon, and Ireland. A great number of copper works, as well as other industries gave the town its commercial importance. Fr. Plowden first established a place of worship for Roman Catholics in Swansea in about 1797, and must therefore be regarded as the founder of the first mission in Glamorgan in modern times. Sent from Bristol to undertake missionary work in Swansea, he took 'a lease for seven years of a room in an old church formerly belonging to the Knights Templar, in the town of Swansea and converted it into a chapel'[2]. This small chapel is probably the 'almost dilapidated building' described in the *New Swansea Guide* of 1823, as belonging to the 'Knights of Jerusalem', and used for Roman Catholic worship[3]. It was located in the Plas House, a fourteenth-century mansion which had once belonged to the Herbert family, and which later was owned by Revd Calvert Richard Jones. In the *Guide to Swansea* of 1802, a list of religious meeting houses concludes with the entry 'At the Place - Roman Catholics'.

Fr. Plowden had great hopes in the near future for this mission if a chapel with a resident priest was to be established. He gave his reason:

> It being a large trading town and much frequented by the Irish, there was a great probability of the establishment increasing, so as to be a good and permanent mission.[4]

He hoped that Swansea, with its own resident priest, would develop as a missionary centre, keeping in touch with the Catholics in mid-Glamorgan, and the scattered Catholic communities far to the west.

From the end of 1805 until the autumn of 1808, the Swansea mission was served by Revd James Sumner, who, for some reason, went under the name of Richards in Swansea. When he left the town, sometime before September 1808, Revd Abbé Séjan, a French refugee who had established himself in Swansea since 1804, assumed the care of the struggling church in the town.

By 28 September 1808, Fr. Séjan was officially in charge of the Swansea mission, describing himself in the first entry of the old Swansea register, in a baptism of that date, as 'A priest of Paris, now taking the place of parish priest in the Catholic Chapel of Swansea'[5]. Although the registers of the church at this date had officially begun in 1811, a Fr. Spooner had inserted three earlier entries belonging to the years 1805 and 1806, which contain two Irish names, Letitia Conners and John Donegan. There was only one marriage entry during the period 1808 to1814, that of James Roarke, aged twenty-seven to Catherine Richards, aged twenty-four, at which Abbé Séjan officiated on 16 May 1813. The name of one of the witnesses was a Thomas Meany. The new Swansea chapel was opened sometime in 1813, although it had already been used for a baptism in November 1812. There seems to be a certain amount of confusion as to the exact location of this establishment, for some authorities state that it was situated in Nelson Terrace, while others give the address as Nelson Place (see Fig. 3). According to the Swansea Corporation Rate Book of 1842 the address is given as Nelson Place. It was the first Catholic Chapel built in Glamorgan in the nineteenth century.

Figure 3: Ruin of the old Swansea Chapel in Nelson Place. *Engraved from a rough sketch kept at the Royal Institution by Miss K. Huntley, Cardiff. The priest lived in no. 5 Nelson Place, probably one of those seen in the picture.*

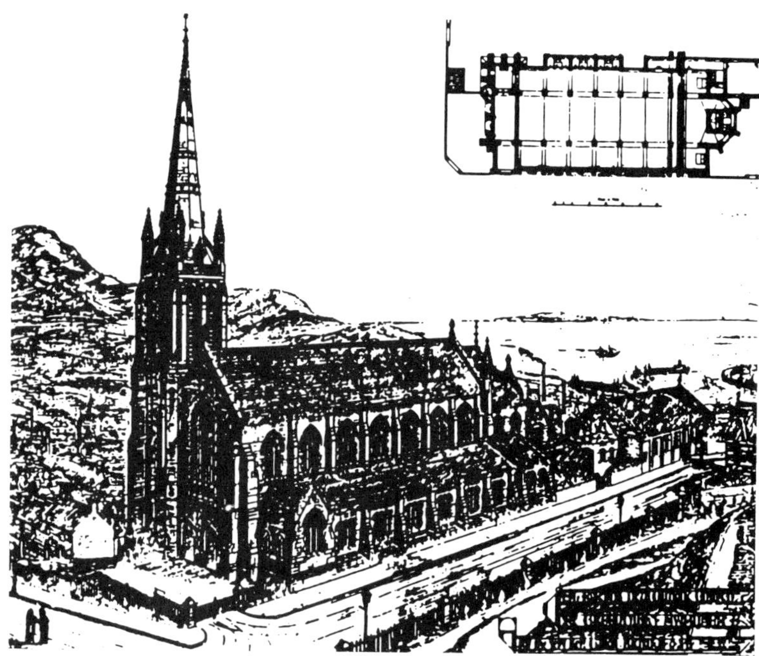

Figure 4: Peter Paul Pugin's original design for St Joseph's Church, 1887.

Abbé Séjan's congregation amounted to a dozen members only, and he maintained himself by teaching French. He had formerly been confessor to Louis XVI, and on the downfall of Bonaparte in 1814, he returned to France. From 1814 until 1824 Swansea was without a resident priest and had to rely on Fr. John Williams who travelled from Brecon, forty miles away, over the mountains.[6] The mission was also occasionally administered from 1817 to1824 by Revd Edward Richards, of Abergavenny.[7] From 1824 until 1839 Swansea had a rapid succession of priests: Revd James Fleetwood (1824-29), James Tuomey (1829-30), Samuel Walsh (1830-31), Robert Platt (1831-32), Michael O'Connor (1832-33), James Butterfield (1833-35), and George Bond (1835-39). Ever since the incumbency of Revd James Fleetwood, the line of Swansea pastors has never been broken. At the end of his ministry in 1829 the congregation in the town did not amount to more than thirty members. but in a census of 1838 by Bishop Baines, there were 400 Catholics at Swansea, and a total of

6,519 for the whole of the Welsh District.

It was not surprising, therefore that in a Brief, dated 3 July 1840, Pope Gregory XVI announced a reorganization of the Catholic Church in England and Wales. The number of districts was increased from four to eight, and a new diocese, called the Welsh District, was carved out of the unwieldy Western District. The new area comprised the thirteen Welsh counties, together with the English county of Herefordshire. In October 1840 Dr Thomas Joseph Brown, OSB, was made Vicar Apostolic of the Welsh District, and was consecrated bishop at Bath. He had hitherto been the Prior of the Benedictine Community at Downside, near Bath.

Before returning to the subject of the Church in Swansea it is worth reflecting on the immense changes which had occurred between October 1773, when Mgr. Charles Walmesley, Vicar Apostolic of the Western District had reported to Rome that there were only 750 Catholics in the whole of Wales, and October 1840, when the figure was between six and seven thousand. In Wales this meant an increase of 735 per cent, which occurred even before the great influx of Irish famine refugees in the late 1840s. The Great Famine in Ireland, which started in 1845 and culminated in 1847, caused millions of Irish people to die of hunger or else emigrate overseas. Thousands were to settle in Swansea during the following decades, and it was this massive influx of Irish people that was to tranform the fortunes of the Roman Catholic Church in Swansea.

In 1839, the Swansea Baptismal Register showed only twenty-seven entries, but by 1852 the number had increased to 159, by which time Aberafan and Neath were no longer included in the parish, warranting a priest of their own. In 1839, when Fr. Charles Kavanagh arrived in Swansea from Newport, he had found the parish very extensive in area, including Aberafan, Neath and Llanelli as well as Swansea. Peter Collins and Peter O'Neill, two Irishmen living in Llanelli, wrote asking for a priest to visit them more often, instead of once a month. Mass was performed in Llanelli in a private house in Old Castle Road, where a Mrs Griffin kept a school. During his early days in the Swansea area, Fr. Kavanagh would be accompanied by a member of the parish for protection, and one by the name of McCarthy rendered this service between Neath and Swansea. He showed himself to be active in attending to the parishioners' needs as well as their spiritual ones. For instance,

Plates 4 and 5: St Joseph's Cathedral, Greenhill, June 1989.

> The cholera epidemic of 1849 showed Fr. Kavanagh in a very good light. His charity embraced all; and his extraordinary labours during the epidemic will never be forgotten. Day and night he spent his time amongst the stricken, ministering to every want, and performing the most menial tasks for the sick and the dying. He in fact lived in the midst of his suffering Irish parishioners, having rented a room in the locality of Greenhill, which even as early as 1849 was called 'Little Ireland'. He was required too, to act as an interpreter for his people, for many of them spoke only the Gaelic, and in Gaelic he conducted his Sunday School,[8]

This Sunday School was situated at the corner of Brook Street and Well Street. A public tribute of thanks, in the form of an address, signed by magistrates, clergy of various denominations, and other gentlemen, and a purse of about fifty or sixty guineas was paid to him as a token of appreciation of the zeal and Christian self-sacrifice which he manifested during the epidemic, irrespective of whether the sufferers were Roman Catholic or otherwise.[9]

Apart from his obvious religious concerns, Fr. Kavanagh was also deeply interested in educational developments on behalf of his parishioners. He had two schools built for the parish, one in Greenhill and the other near St David's Church, in Rutland Place, which was opened on 8 September 1847. The school at Greenhill was called, aptly enough, St Patrick's, and was the successor of the earlier Sunday school mentioned above. The school near St David's Church was built four years after the erection of the church itself, in 1851. Fr. Kavanagh was also one of the founders of the Royal Institution of South Wales, and was an active member of Literary Association connected with the Institution; he frequently delivered lectures, and until his missionary work became too heavy, gave lessons to young men. After the course of seventeen years' ministry, he died on 20 October 1856, aged forty-seven. He was the first person to be buried in the new cemetery at Danygraig, the progress of which he had taken such a great interest in before his death.

By 1851, the Welsh District had been divided, by the creation of two new dioceses, both containing English counties. The six northern counties of Wales were annexed to the diocese of Shrewsbury, while the counties of South Wales together with Herefordshire were regrouped to form the diocese of Newport and Menevia. It is possible to gauge the strength of the roman Catholic Church in Swansea, by the numbers attending mass on a particular Sunday in 1851 by using the returns of the religious census compiled in that year. It provides us with the following statistical information:

Church accommodation, free 200; other 12; standing 200
Present, Morning 300; Evening 200
Average (12 months): General Congregation 350; scholars 200.

The 1851 religious census was compiled at a time when the Irish famine immigration was in full flood, but it was not until the civil census of 1861 that the highest number of Irish-born people was recorded in Wales. The estimated number of Irish-born people in Swansea and in the Swansea area in 1851 was 1,369. Eight years later we are supplied with this information:

> The congregation is a large one, but consists chiefly of Irish people. Out of 3,000 residents in Swansea (in 1859) who, it is computed, belong to the Roman Catholic faith, probably some 2,800 are Irish. It is indeed, the immigration of the Irish that has raised the cause here to its present position.

The writer continued:

> There are three services during the day at the chapel, and different congregations assemble on each occasion. The chapel will hold about 350 people only. The congregation was for the most part composed of the labouring classes and the very poor - anongst whom Irish features largely predominate.

But he also added 'There were some persons of respectability near where I sat.'

From the above evidence, it will be seen that there was a tremendous increase in the number of Irish-born people in Swansea between 1851 and 1859, and likewise a growth in the number of Roman Catholics in the town. This remarkable development was witnessed by Fr. Kavanagh during his seventeen-year ministry, which lasted up to his death in 1856. He was succeeded by Revd Peter Lewis, a Welsh speaker, the author of a book entitled *Ymddiddan am Grefydd rhwng Thomas a William*. He also served the church for a period of seventeen years, and his labours were shared by Revd Thomas Fenn. Just before his death in 1856, Fr. Kavanagh had applied to Swansea Town Council for a lease of land at Greenhill for the erection of a schoolroom, although negotiations for this were not complete when he died. It was left to his successor, Fr. Lewis, who applied for a lease of land in June 1857, and on 18 August 1857, he asked for more land on which to build a house, which subsequently became the site of St Mary's Convent. In 1862, a small group of Ursuline Sisters, who had first come to Swansea two years before, moved into the completed convent, and over the next few years two school buildings were erected.

When they first came to Swansea on 19 October 1860, the Ursulines lived at no. 3 Rutland Street. On 12 June 1862, they moved into the new convent. Their zeal and influence went a long way to make up for the absence of a resident priest in Greenhill. The convent had about a dozen sisters of the Order of Ursulines, some of whom were Breton and some Irish. They were affiliated to the Mother House of Chavègnes en Pailliers near Nantes, and were introduced to Swansea by Bishop Brown. He had the idea, that being Breton, the affinity of their speech with the Welsh language might be a means of bringing about the conversion of Wales, which was an aspiration dear to his heart. The idea was a noble one, but though the languages were akin, in practical terms the speech was mutually unintelligable.

The Sisters Ursulines of Jesus, were founded by the venerable Louis Marie Baudouin, at Chavègnes en Pailliers in the diocese of Luçon, Vendée, near Nantes, Brittany, in 1802. In 1834, a congregation of them had been founded in Edinburgh and dedicated to St Margaret. (Incidentally, this was the first convent to be established in Scotland since the Reformation.) The advent of the sisters to Swansea occurred through the energies of Miss Eleanor Lang-Mason, a Scottish lady of considerable means, who had converted to Catholicism. Miss Lang-Mason was acquainted with Bishop Brown, whose Newport diocese at that time incorporated the present Archdiocese of Cardiff. She became an Ursuline of Jesus, entering as a novitiate of the congregation of St Margaret's Convent, Edinburgh, where she was professed as Sister St Sophia. Her wish was to found a mission among a poor Catholic population, and Bishop Brown suggested Swansea. He asked Father Lewis, who was then at St David's Parish, Swansea to escort some nuns from Brittany to Swansea. The house which they occupied in Rutland Street was later used as a booking office for the Mumbles railway.[10] There the sisters remained until the Convent of St Mary's was built in Greenhill in 1862. Using the house in Rutland Street as their base, the sisters conducted classes, for both boys and girls, among the recently established Catholic Irish population in the district of Greenhill. These classes were housed in a room of an old building which at the time occupied the site of the present boys' school. The sisters also visited the sick and needy in their homes.

By 1864, the estimated congregation was 1,000, Father Lewis named the following people who had assisted him: James Murray, Thomas Flynn, Thomas Elder, Dr Harrington, Daniel O'Connor, Patrick Nolan, Morris Duggan (called the King of Greenhill), a Mr Cady, who was a member of the Board of Guardians, a Mr Daniels, and also Messrs Bagshaw, Butler, Young and Fitzgerald.[11]

In 1865, the foundations for the first church at Greenhill were laid, and this building was formally opened at the end of 1866. The original church lay to the south of the present one, and since 1888 has served as the church hall.

Father Lewis waged a constant war upon the drinking dens and dance saloons which he called 'hotbeds of vice and iniquity'. He did succeed in closing one place, and from the pulpit one Sunday made this triumphant announcement:

> James Quinn, like a true Irishman, has listened to the advice of his clergy, and has stopped dancing in his house.

Father Lewis retired in 1873,[12] and his departure heralded a change.

The Swansea mission, had hitherto been served entirely from St David's, but on the retirement of Father Lewis, in 1873, Bishop Brown placed it in the charge of the English Benedictine congregation. St David's was raised to the status of a missionary priory, and continued to be the residence of the clergy. Greenhill was served from St David's. Father Hurworth took charge of this outlying district and said mass there daily. St Joseph's therefore was possessed of church, convent and schools, but its rapidly increasing congregation could no longer be left without a resident pastor of their own. This state of affairs was to be remedied in the middle years of the 1870s.

On 26 October 1873, the Benedictine Fathers took over charge of the Swansea mission and Canon Price was sent as the new pastor. At this time the parish was divided into two districts; that of St Joseph's was considered to be north of a line drawn between Croft Street and Thomas Street, that of St David's, south of this line. Effectively, this meant that St Joseph's separated from the mother church of St David's, and at the end of November 1875, was made an independent mission. Canon Revd J. Wulstan Richards was placed in charge, on 8 December, 1875, while Canon Wilson took care of St David's. Father

Richards rented a four-room workingman's house in Llangyfelach Terrace as his first presbytery. Years later, he described his new parish thus:

> Greenhill was a new working men's district in the process of formation, and on whose bleak and bare hillside where roads and streets had yet to be made, undrained and unlighted.

Father Richards found in Greenhill an absence of bigotry amongst the Welsh people, and a good understanding between them and their Irish neighbours. A Catholic priest was received everywhere with respect. Though on friendly terms with their Welsh neighbours, the quarter where the Irish dwelt was a 'Little Ireland' of itself, where its people lived their own lives and followed their own national customs with absolute freedom and independence. Socially they were all equal, being all men of 'the labouring class'. The skilled labour was practically monopolised by the Welsh. On St Patrick's Day there was always a procession from St David's or St Joseph's through the main streets to the Assembly Rooms in Cambrian Place. There were the 'Hibernian Minstrels', who met in one or other of the schoolrooms for practice, and gave frequent concerts to raise funds for the parish. When there was distress in Ireland in 1862, £26 was readily collected from St David's and Greenhill to feed their needy countrymen.[13]

Father Richards's helpers included the two Retikens, Kiely, Turner, Appleyard, Troy, Tracy, Holly, Curwin, O'Brien, Clancy, Kinealy, Stafford, Green, Bolan and Jerry O'Shea. Yet, although from the same country, they had distinct types of character recalling the counties from which they came. The Wexford men were not true Celts, but descendants of English settlers in the Pale, as their names, Turner, Clarke, Stafford, Russell, Tracy, indicated. These mostly kept themselves apart from the other Irish in Greenhill. The Waterford men were more numerous, and, with their neighbours from Tipperary, formed a fine body of men, of splendid physique, and of Scandinavian origin and type. But the greatest number, by far, hailed from Cork and its neighbourhood. These were of purely Celtic origin and character.[14] However, as Richards remarked, there was one unifying factor:

> The old grandmothers who had come from Ireland were the one conservative element in the flock, the one link between the old life and the new. They were the ones with faith and piety, the folk-lore and the wake-ceremonial, and of Irish poetry and language. They always wore the ancestral cloak around them in church. In confessional they were known by their voice and speed. 'Please,

> Canon, I can only confess in Irish'. They had the very accents of the long ages of faith of Catholic Ireland, and of a long-suffering race.[15]

The idea of building a newer, bigger church had been in Canon Richards's mind for some time, thus when six leasehold cottages adjoining the Presbytery came up for sale, he arranged for them to be bought by a purchaser seemingly unconnected with the church. Other adjacent plots were acquired soon afterwards. An application was then made to the Town Council, and the freehold reversion was granted to the church authorities. Having received permission to build from the Provinicial of the English Benedictine Congregation, Canon Richards invited Peter Paul Pugin, the renowned church architect, to design the new building.[16] The foundation stone of the new church was laid by the Bishop of Newport and Menevia on 2 October 1886. The work was completed within two years, and the building was formally opened by the bishop on 27 September 1888. A century later it was made into the Cathedral of the newly-created diocese of Menevia (see plates 4 and 5). This was a suitable culmination of two centuries of Roman Catholic growth in Swansea, brought about predominantly by the masses of Irish who entered Swansea during the nineteenth century, especially in the post-famine decades.

NOTES

1. J.M.C. Cronin, 'Itinerant Missionaries in Glamorgan in the eighteenth century', in *St Peter's Magazine*, iv, no. 8 (1924), pp.228-33.
2. 'Father Plowden's missionary work at Swansea', in *SPM*, ix (1929), p.43.
3. ibid., p.43.
4. ibid., p.44.
5. *Sundays in Wales, by a Week-Day Preacher*, p.19.
6. J.M.C. Cronin, 'Catholicism in Glamorgan before 1820', in *SPM*, ix (1929), p.111.
7. *Sundays in Wales*, p.20.
8. Revd Fr. G. Spencer, *Catholic Life in Swansea* (Swansea, 1947).
9. The *Cambrian*, 21 December 1849.
10. *Centenary of St Mary's Convent, Greenhill, Swansea, 1862-1962*.
11. Spencer, *Catholic Life in Swansea*.
12. ibid.
13. J.W. Richards, *Reminiscences of the Early Days of the Parish and Church of St Joseph's, Greenhill, Swansea*.
14. ibid.
15. ibid.
16. *St Joseph's Church and Greenhill. A Centenary Exhibition* (Swansea, 1988), p.2.

CHAPTER THREE

Greenhill as reflected in the Health Reports of the 1840s and 1850s

The Health Reports of 1845, 1849, 1854 and 1856, are valuable sources on the living conditions of the Irish population of Greenhill. The Greenhill area had a higher density of Irish inhabitants than any other part of Swansea, even before the mass influx into the town of Irish famine immigrants from the late 1840s. From the mid-nineteenth century onwards it was known as 'Little Ireland'. Swansea's industrial area had developed to the north of the town, dominated by copper works, the Morfa and the Hafod works, amongst others. One result of this industrial growth was to create a distinctive, nucleus of working-class housing in close proximity to the works, given that walking to work was the only means of movement. These groupings of working-class housing were associated with Neath Road, Llangyfelach Road, and Carmarthen Road, the three main roads which led out of Swansea towards the north and west. At the point where these three lines merged into High Street, at the edge of the growing shopping and business centre, there was the poorest quality slum housing, and there, too, was the major grouping of Irish immigrants in Swansea, in the locality known as Greenhill.[1] It was wedged in between the districts of Waun Wen and Hafod, which were overwhelmingly non-Irish.

Before studying in detail the information on the terrible living conditions to be found in this locality, furnished by the health reports, it is well to remember that the living conditions of the Irish peasantry were far from a rural idyll. In the summer of 1809, Lewis Weston Dillwyn, the proprietor of the Cambrian pottery, and a notable

Swansea figure, visited the south-western counties of Ireland, and his comments on the living conditions of the mass of the rural Irish are worth noting. They are as good a description as any of the hardships endured by the Irish in the early nineteenth century. Fortunately, his diary has been preserved in the archives of Trinity College, Dublin.[2] In his diary entry dated, Saturday, 8 June 1809, he noted:

> The want of a middle rank struck me forcibly as we rode along for we rarely saw any houses that were not either the villas of gentlemen or the most wretched hovels, and the people were generally either well dressed or clothed in rags.

On Friday, 14 July he elaborated on his general observations of the previous month,

> I had often heard of the wretchedness of an Irish cabin, but had no idea that any of them were so wretched as are most of those which we passed this day. They are built with mud roofed turf, and have rarely any window whatever. Some of them are without any chimney and in others the smoke is let out by a hole cut in the roof. The insides were generally filled with smoke of which we frequently observed more issuing from the door than from the chimney. We are told that these poor wretches prefer a room when thus filled, and think it warmer and more comfortable.

One final entry he made on Thursday, 1 August 1809 is also worth noting, as a comment on the Irish respect for 'English Law'!

> At Mill Street as in every other town and village there is a Barrack for two or three companies of Infantry, it having been found that no law can be enforced in Ireland without the assistance of a Bayonet.

When the Great Famine came to Ireland during the second half of the 1840s, the living conditions of the landless Irish country-dweller were basically the same as those described by Dillwyn in 1809. The tragic story of the Famine and its effects are too well known to be retold, but it is sufficient to remember that the pre-famine population of Ireland was approaching nine million, and that this figure was halved within a decade. Millions starved, while millions emigrated. The Irish emigration to America has captured the imagination to a greater extent than the less spectacular movement from Ireland to Britain. However, in the last twenty years, there have been several studies of the Irish communities throughout England, Scotland and Wales. One thing is clear about the Irish migration to Britain: there were three distinct entry points for the Irish. First, there was the Clyde entry, which brought considerable numbers from Ulster to Glasgow,

Edinburgh, and other parts of Scotland. Secondly, there was the important port of Liverpool, receiving Irish from Dublin and its hinterland, as well as from the province of Connaught, Thirdly, and of greatest relevance to this study, the South Wales ports and Bristol. The vast majority of Irish immigrants using the southern entries were from County Cork, followed by Irish from the adjacent counties of Kerry, Limerick, Tipperary, and Waterford. A large number also came from Wexford and Clare, fewer from the inland counties of the south, and fewer still from Connaught and Ulster. This is also borne out by studies of the Bristol Irish[3], and is further discussed in Chapter V.

Figure 5: 'A Funeral at Skibbereen'. A sketch made by a Mr Smyth of Cork during the Famine.

Figure 6: Desolation in Skibbereen, Co. Cork, 1848

The Health Reports of 1845, 1849, 1854 and 1856 describe in detail the living conditions which the Irish immigrants to Greenhill had to endure. Furthermore, the horrifying sanitary conditions were successively exposed by Sir Henry T. de la Beche in 1845 in the *(Health of Towns Commission) Report on the State of Bristol, Bath, Frome, Swansea, Merthyr Tydfil and Brecon*; by George Thomas Clark in his *Report to the General Board of Health* of 1849; by William Henry Michael in his *Supplementary Report on the Cholera in Swansea in 1849*, which was published in 1854, and finally, *The Health Report* of 1856, also by W.H. Michael.

These reports give valuable, graphic accounts of the particularly bad conditions to be found on the northern outskirts of the borough of Swansea, as well as in the overcrowded courts and alleys that were to be found in High Street and the Strand. They are worth quoting in full where they relate specifically to the Irish locality of Greenhill.

The greatest proportion of deaths in Swansea caused by outbreaks of cholera and typhus epidemics between 1839 and 1842 occurred in the Strand and Greenhill localities. In 1849, the cholera epidemic was confined to the upper part of the town (see Map 7), particularly in the vicinity of Greenhill. W.H. Michael, the first Medical Officer of Health estimated that no less than seventeen per cent of the total number of deaths for the whole of Swansea occurred in this area.

The earliest surviving report is Sir Henry T. de la Beche's *(Health of Towns Commission) Report of the State of Bristol, Bath, Frome, Swansea, Merthyr Tydfil and Brecon,* published in 1845. The section relating to Swansea is covered by pages 57 to 76, and is graphic in the extreme. For instance, on page 63 he stated:

> In the year 1839, I find in a Report of the Royal Institution of South Wales, the following statement:- Town of Swansea (within the Turn-pike-gates).
> Houses/Offices, etc.: 1,859
> Hotels/Inns/Public Houses/Beer houses: 162
> Vacant Houses: 144
> Churches: 2
> Chapels: 17
> Lodging Houses:- These are numerous, and present the usual characteristics of over-crowding, bad ventilation, and want of cleanliness. In Dr Bird's answers he presents us with the following account of 'lodging houses', and their inhabitants, given him by the Inspector of Police for Swansea:-
>
> Mr. W. Rees feels since there are 60 low lodging houses or beggar-hotels in this town; in some of these he has seen 16 persons sleeping in the same room, Irish,

> Scotch, and Welsh, consisting of wives, husbands, children and single people, all in the same room. He has seen 6 or 7 in the same bed, i.e., a man, his wife, and children. These lodgers pay from 2d to 3d per night, before they go to bed. Mr Rees thinks there must be from 250-300 of the commonest prostitutes at Swansea. They are very debauched in their habits as regards drink; many of them sleep on straw in a corner of the room, whilst they allow ordure to cover the floor, or throw it with the ashes; so dirty are their domestic habits. In some cases, several take a small house together, whilst others live in lodgings. There are many prostitutes of a better kind; these are more decent in their habits and dwellings.

He concluded his report by giving the total number of deaths for each locality for the years 1839-1842:

> In the years from 1839 to 1842 the greatest proportion of deaths have taken place in the Strand: 108; Greenhill and upper district: 524 and Middle district: 342, the very situations in which there exist no sewerage, and in which three out of four have been fever inflaminatory cases. The comparison between these districts and others inhabited by the same class has with due regard to the proportion of the population, occupied my attention, and the result has been a conviction of the evils arising from the want of a proper system of drainage, sewerage, and cleansing.

Classification of Deaths at Swansea for the years 1839-1842.

High Street	93
Strand	108
Green Hill	524
Middle	342
Burrows	23
Upper suburbs	62
Sketty	36
Mount Pleasant	19
St Thomas	38
Others	33
Total:	1,278

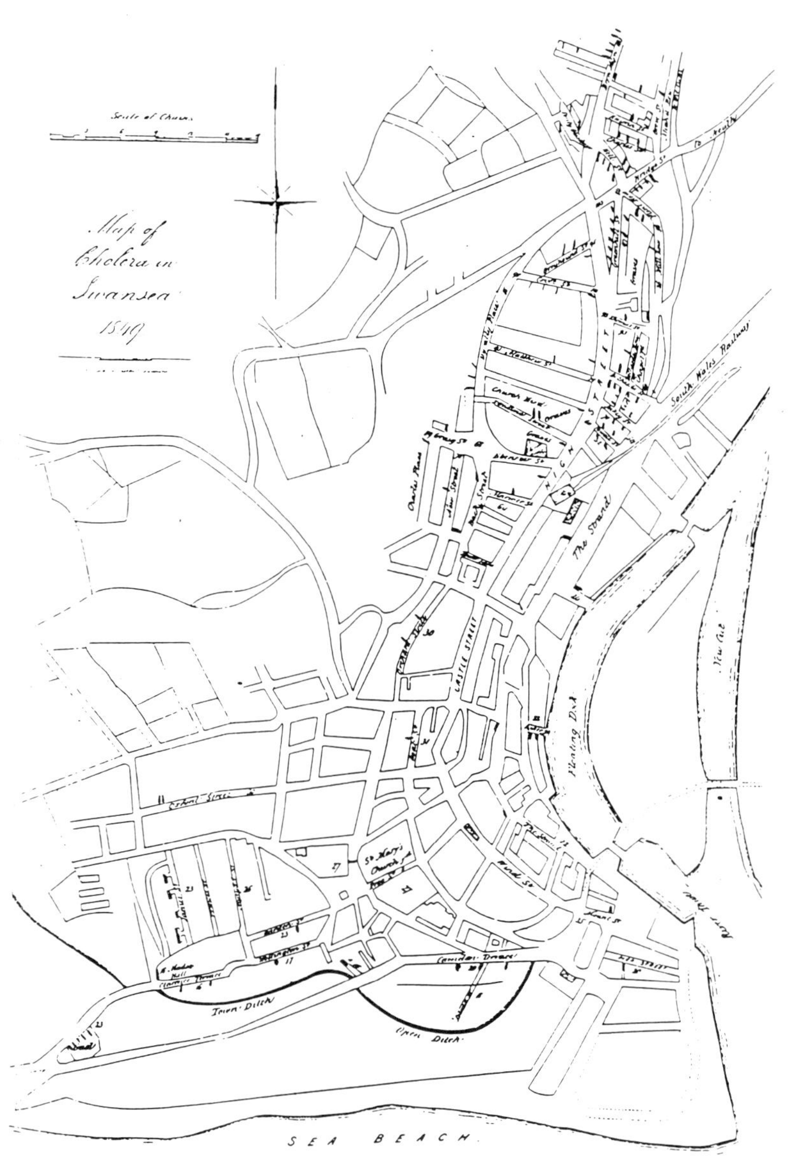

Map 7: Map of Cholera in Swansea, 1849.

The second report was prepared by George Thomas Clark in 1849, and entitled *Report to the General Board of Health on a Preliminary Inquiry into the Sewerage, Drainage, and Supply of Water, and the Sanitary Condition of the Inhabitants of the Town and Borough of Swansea, under the Public Health Act* (11 and 12 Vict. *cap*. 63).

The report began in a very factual mode. For example, it noted that

> Mr Michael John Michael was Mayor of Swansea in the 1840s. In 1841, according to the census, there were in the borough of Swansea 3,166 houses inhabited, and 203 empty or building. 7,861 males and 8,926 females. The total population being then 16,787. In 1849 it is presumed to be between 19,000 and 20,000.

He further explained his *modus operandi:*

> My inquiries necessarily led me into those parts of the town and suburb of Swansea which lie outside of the franchise, though within the borough, and I found the groups of population clustered about the several works and upon the left bank of the Tawe, so connected with each other and with the town, that it became very evident that it would be unadvisable, no less on sanitary than on economical considerations, to exclude any part of the borough from the operation of the Act, an opinion which I found to be in unison with that generally expressed juring the inquiry.

His first reference to Greenhill mentioned a 'cellar dwelling', of the type well known in the slum areas of the larger cities in this period:

> In Bridge Street is a room half underground, as far as I could learn the only place in the town at all approaching the condition of a cellar dwelling. It is inhabitated by an Irish family, who rent it at 1s. a week.

He went on to describe this area in general terms:

> I proceed to notice, in the first place, the worst parts of Swansea. These are probably about the northern end of High Street and Greenhill, and their subordinate courts, especially the district known as Little Ireland.
> Referring to Green Row, Mr Davis reports that there are 3 houses, of two rooms each, without privies or sewers; he adds, 'I have been informed that as many as 30 have lodged the same night in one of these cottages. They are a nuisance to the neighbourhood'.

He had this to say about Well Street:

> In and about Well Street the houses are bad, the people chiefly Irish and much crowded together, and the streets and yards unpaved or illpaved, and in a filthy state . . .

> In Dyvatty Place is the public slaughter house. Opposite to the slaughter house is a row of houses in a filthy condition, with offensive pig-styes, etc.

and continuing in his description of the same locality he noted that

> The public springs of Swansea are at Dyvatty Pystil, the Washing Lake and also the Glas Dwr Brook, at Greenhill.

This report has added interest, as it describes the stage of the upper part of the town on the eve of the cholera epidemic of 1849.

The report of 1854 by W.H. Michael, the Medical Officer for the Swansea Local Board of Health, contained a Supplementary Report on cholera in Swansea in 1849. This report was known as the *First Quarterly Report on the Sickness and Mortality of the Borough of Swansea* from 1 October 1853, to 1 January 1854. In the Supplementary Report on cholera, he began by suggesting that the return of cholera to Swansea in the Autumn of 1853, would strike in the same localities of the town again, i.e., Greenhill, Strand, etc., if precautions were not taken:

> Gentlemen,
>
> The advent of Epidemic Cholera to this country in the Autumn of 1853, and the similarity of its course to what occurred in 1848, makes it particularly at this juncture my duty to furnish you with some information relative to the visitation which this town experienced in 1849 . . . .
>
> I beg, therefore, to furnish you with a list of the deaths which occurred in this Borough, from the 18th day of July 1849, to the 9th day of October, 1849, with the localities in which the deaths occurred, that should we again unhappily be visited by this pestilence, that is where we should expect to find it again locating itself and expending its strength, for it is in this part of the town we find fever, or any other epidemic, if at all present in the district, dealing out death to the inhabitants of the dirty, ill-drained, and close habitations with which this part of the town abounds, and where an entire absence of water renders cleanliness, comfort, or health, almost unattainable.

Map 7 shows clearly where the greatest number of deaths occurred in the cholera epidemic of 1849.

By 1856, Michael was no longer Medical Officer of the Swansea Local Board of health, but he was responsible for *The Medical Report on the Sickness and Mortality of the Borough of Swansea for the Year 1854, together with Maps and Appendix.*

He began by describing the administrative framework of the town:

> The Municipal Borough of Swansea, made into a District under the Public Health Acts comprises, 1st the Town proper, being part of the parish of Swansea and the whole of the parish of St John, and, 2ndly, parts of the parishes of Llansamlet and Llangyfelach. These portions of the borough are included in three separate Registration Districts. At the census of 1851, 22,675 inhabitants belonged to Swansea, 1,215 to St John, 3,496 to Llansamlet, and 4,075 to Llangyfelach.

On page 18, he turned his attention to the Greenhill locality (see Map 8):

> I have hitherto made no allusion to the Greenhill district, because I am unable to give you accurate statistics of its mortality, the deaths being for the most part registered as occurring in 'Greenhill', the name of the street not being added. Thus, in the 5 years ending December 31st 1853, 143 cases of deaths have no other address. But it is evident, from the fact that all Epidemics locate themselves in this district, and their severity always being there increased, that this part of town must be considered the most in want of measures of sanitary reform.
>
> I had the honour, in 1853, to report to you 'that this district, during the prevalence of Cholera in 1849, was severely visited, almost every house beyond the old turnpike gate, in Well Street, Angel Court, Llangyfelach Street, Charles Street, Emma Street, and Ann Street, having had its inmates more or less affected by the Epidemic'.
>
> Thickly peopled, with no drainage or efficient water-supply, the houses are filthy, and in many cases unfit for human habitation, heaps of ashes filling up the backyards, privies and cesspools in a filthy and unprotected condition.
>
> Drains, where they exist at the back of houses (Charles Street and Llangyfelach Street), black and stagnant, and filthy, in almost every case open, and, where they are not open, in so bad a state of repair, as rather to aggravate their pestilential condition, by penning up foul gases, and concentrating them until they become doubly poisonous.
>
> The courts are so constantly immersed in water as to be almost always muddy and unwholesome. In many of these houses, in addition to the ordinary inmates, several lodgers are accommodated; and this in the midst of filth, with the entire absence of ventilation, cannot fail to engender and intensify epidemic disease, which is not only felt here, but, as from a focus, radiates over every other portion of the town. Neither are the inhabitants deterred from adding to these evils (except by incessant vigilance on the part of your Officers), by keeping pigs, horses, cows, asses, poultry, etc., in or immediately contiguous to their houses, in the small court-yards attached, by courtesy called gardens, from which, instead of nature's odorous perfume, arise ever nauseous and sickening smells.

> It is with pleasure I refer you to the fact, that during my year of office, no death or case of epidemic disease has occurred in the common lodging-houses of this town, but as there are but 11 registered houses, having accommodation for 96 inmates, it must therefore of necessity follow, with the large number of 'navvies' and other casual labourers employed in the town and neighbourhood, that but few can be acommodated in these lodgings, the great mass crowding into the houses of their friends in Charles Street, Llangyfelach Street, and neighbourhood, to the great detriment of the sanitary condition of the Borough.
> . . . for it cannot be otherwise than that, while overcrowding engenders disease, the promiscuous huddling together of the sexes should encourage and invite crime. The one helps to fill our Workhouse, and the other our Gaol.

In 1854, Dr Thomas Williams, in his *Report on Copper Smoke*, which he submitted to the Local Board of Health, wrote:

> To the very large numbers of breadless, homeless immigrants from Ireland such cottages (as were found at Greenhill) as these were palaces.

While this may be an exaggeration, it is plain from Lewis Weston Dillwyn's description of the houses of the Irish peasantry quoted at the beginning of this chapter, that the living conditions of the poor in rural Ireland left much to be desired. From the reports of the 1840s and 1850s it is clear that there was an extreme health problem in the Greenhill locality owing to an inadequate water supply, coupled with gross overcrowding. The number of people in each household can be judged from the data gathered from the civil censuses of 1841, 1851, and 1861 (see Appendix). The series of articles entitled 'A visit to the Courts and Alleys of Swansea' from the *Cambrian* newspaper of 1853, underlines the seriousness of the problem.

NOTES

1. H. Carter, 'The Structure of Glamorgan Towns in the Nineteenth Century', in *GCH*, vi, *Glamorgan Society, 1780-1980*, ed, P. Morgan (Cardiff, 1989).
2. G.J. Lyne, 'Lewis Dillwyn's Visit to Waterford, Cork and Tipperary in 1809', in *JCHAS*, xli No. 50 (1986).
3. D. Large, 'Irish in Bristol in 1851: A Census Enumeration', in *The Irish in the Victorian City*, ed. R. Swift.

CHAPTER FOUR

The Irish as reported in the Swansea Newspapers of the 1840s and 1850s

The newspaper reports relating to the Irish and the Irish community of Greenhill in this chapter are extracted mainly from the *Cambrian* newspaper of the 1840s and1850s. However, the *Swansea Journal* for the year 1843, and the Welsh language periodical, *Y Diwygiwr* for 1848 have also been consulted.

Some of the earliest Irish material in the *Cambrian* relates to happenings elsewhere, such as the outbreak of fighting between a Welsh and an Irish regiment at Woolwich Barracks in 1804[1] or a fight between Welsh and Irish workers at the Varteg Iron Works, Pontypool in 1834.[2] The earliest items relating to the Irish in Swansea begin to appear in the *Cambrian* in the period from about 1818 to 1825, and are related to the passing of Irish counterfeit coins. Indeed, from the 1840s Irish-related material becomes more evident, much of it being found in the Police Intelligence and the Petty Sessions columns.

However, none of the local newspapers, from the beginning of the nineteenth century to the 1860s, and even in the 1840s and 1850s contains any reports of anti-Irish riots or similar occurrences in Swansea, although, at various times in the nineteenth century, there were several such riots in other parts of South Wales where the Irish settled in great numbers, as at Cardiff, Pontypool and Tredegar. The only evidence of Welsh workers attacking Irish workers, is to be gleaned from the diary of Lewis Weston Dillwyn for Thursday, 19 July 1826.

Drove to Swansea chiefly on Magisterial Business to protect some Irishmen who have been employed in the Rose Copperworks, and who the other men have violently driven off. Committed the two chief offenders one for two and the other for one month to hard labour[3]

But despite the lack of evidence in the newspapers for any large scale anti-Irish disturbances, there were two incidents during the 1840s which are worth recording, as they give us an insight into the potential underlying tensions that existed between the Welsh and Irish in this period. They were both murder cases. The first was committed on Tuesday, 16 August 1842, when six Welshmen murdered an Irishman, John Bowling. The other incident occurred on Tuesday, 9 May 1848, and concerned the murder of two Welshmen by a party of Irishmen. The *Cambrian* of August 20 1842 gave a graphic account;

Horrid and Wilful Murder at Swansea - On Tuesday morning last, the 16th instant, the greatest excitement prevailed in the town, caused by the report that a man had been murdered early that morning, in Bethesda Street, by five others; and that two persons who had gone to his assistance, were so severely beaten as to place their lives in imminent danger.

At the extremity of a narrow, ill ventilated passage, in a wretched hovel, scarcely tenantable for pigs, we discovered the body of a young man. In a neighbouring cottage a poor man, named Connor was sitting in a chair, in a helpless condition.

At 1'o'clock in the morning, five men entered the court, which was principally inhabited by Irishmen and their families, and said that they were looking for women. When an Irishman wanted to know why they had come to the area, he was told: 'We will let you know b . . . y Pat', and the Irishman was laid low. Honoria Connor, wife of the Irishman was a witness as was Timothy Leary, who lived in Bethesda Street, at the back of the 'Elephant and Castle', Wm. Webb a policemen arrested three of the men in a nearby cottage.

The trial took place at the Glamorganshire Lent Assizes, and was reported in a supplement to the *Swansea Journal* of 1 March 1843.

Six men were 'charged with the wilful murder of John Bowling'. They were David Rees, alias Dashy, aged 21, William Thomas, alias, Crib, aged 27, William Davies, alias Will Cox, aged 29, John Evans, alias Johnny the Backward, aged 19, John Lewis, alias Shony Ty Coch, aged 23, and Rees Griffiths, aged 44.

The deceased, John Bowling, was a young Irishman about 24 years of age. He came to reside at Swansea about 1840; and at the time of his death had a wife and two young children. A fortnight before the fatal occurrence, Bowling and his family went to reside in a small passage at Greenhill, in this town, leading out of Bethesda Street. The passage in question contains only seven houses; and it would appear that these houses, with the exception of one, were all tenanted by poor Irish labourers and their families. One was occupied by the prisoner William Davies (Will Cox). Bowling's wife was accosted on her way home from a neighbour's house by William Thomas (Crib) who said - 'You Irish whore, I wish I was in bed with you for half an hour', she repelled him and went into her house, took a piece of brick from the fireplace and struck Thomas on the forehead. He then kicked her once or more, in her face. At this time the remaining five prisoners were in the house of William Davies, which was immediately opposite, and they came over. Just after John Bowling entered the passage from Bethesda Street; and when he got to the corner of his house he addressed the parties present in these words - 'Well, boys, what is all this noise at this time of night'; on which David Rees (Dashy), who had in his hands a hatchet, came up to the deceased and said - 'I will soon let you know you Irish b . . . r'; and with that he struck the deceased on his forehead with a hatchet, and the deceased fell to the ground. All the prisoners then crowded into the house and started kicking Bowling, Rees Griffiths, joining in with the others said 'Let us kill the Irish B . . . r', William Thomas also stabbed the deceased about his neck with a knife.

Honoria Connor was called as a witness, she was the wife of Thomas Connor, and they were neighbours of the Bowling family. She says that she and her husband had lived in the passage for three years and that her neighbours were, a man by the name of Cochrane, another Halloran, Timothy Carey, and Wm. Scantery. Wm. Davies the prisoner also lived there.

Ellen Halloran was then examined. She said that she was the wife of Michael Halloran, and were also neighbours. After the murderers left Bowling's house, she went over and told his wife in Irish so that they could not understand, 'go out and cry murder or else we shall all be killed'. They were then attacking Connor, he was kicked in his private parts.

Timothy Leary also gave evidence, and said that he had been attacked by the same men previously. he claimed that it was after he had threatened to knock their brains out with the hatchet, that they took it from him. 'There was a little fray between me and my old woman, but was that any interference of theirs, was it? I cannot say how many public houses I was in that day - whether fifty or a hundred.. . . I will swear I did not swing the hatchet around my head and say - 'there shall be blood in our court shortly'.

The Court returned a verdict of Manslaughter, and the prisoners were sentenced to be transported beyond the seas for the terms of their natural lives. The judge said that it seems that they had some enmity against John Bowling and his neighbours, because they were all Irish. Catherine Bowling and her two children received money from a collection in order to assist them to return to Ireland.[4]

The other infamous murder case involving a clash between Welsh and Irish happened six years later, and was reported in the *Cambrian*, on 12 May 1848.

Editorial
The Cwrw Bach:- The establishment of those merry meetings, known by the Welsh appelation of cwrw bach. Two brutal murders, and two horrid oaths, have been the concomitants of this nefarious system within a short week.

They have proved a prolific source of immorality, misery, and crime from time to time.

As long as there continues such an influx of Irish and other labourers into the principality, these meetings will prove a place of rendezvous for different labourers engaged on the Railway - Irish, Cornish, and Welsh. After partaking of 'libations deep', the passions are raised, natural antipathies and prejudices find a ready vent - collision.

Dreadful Murder near Swansea!
Tuesday morning last 9 May 1848 the first spot was a small courtyard before a thatched house, known by the Welsh name of Tywyth, at which a merry meeting, called a Cwrw Bach, was held that night. The second spot, on the highway near the entrance to the said courtyard about ten yards from the other spot. Near to it is the public house known by the sign of the Marquis's Arms. The murderers were five Irish excavators, named Patrick Leary, aged 28, Michael Leary, about 40, his brother; Thomas Martin, 28 years, William Norris, aged 18, and his brother, John Norris, 25 years. All of whom had been during the previous week, employed on the South Wales Railway, near Loughor, and from having been residing in and about Swansea from time to time, are well known characters. The victims were John Williams aged 47 and Jenkin Evans, aged 52 who were locals. They were stabbed.

On Monday night, a man named William Davies held a Cwrw Bach near the Marquis, kept by David Evans, the son of Jenkin Evans (victim). Twenty drank till 1 - 2 o'clock in the morning. About 12.30 a party of five Irish 'navvies' entered. They drank 3 quarts of beer. then there was an argument and a fight started between the Irish and the Welsh. The Irishmen used their spades as weapons. After the killings they made off for Greenhill, Swansea. The Irishmen had two spades and two sticks.

William Connor, the fiddler, who had been present, on being examined, sad he had been called to play at the cwrw bach, but getting drunk, he fell asleep, and knew nothing of the affray - but, he seemed to know more!

Patrick Leary on being examined said that a tall Welsh chap had asked him the reason that he was coming to work for the low wages. As the Irishmen ran to Cwmbwrla Gate, Tom Martin had said 'I am the boy that let the wind pass through some of them' They then ran to a house where they were in the habit of lodging - it was next door to Bethesda Chapel.

On the afternoon of Wednesday 10 May 1848, Tom Martin was discovered at the quarry at Red Jacket, Briton Ferry. The other four were captured near Cowbridge by P.S. John Price of Llangyfelach.

Both of these incidents suggest that there was a certain amount of latent ill-feeling between the Irish and the native Welsh at this period. However, it was not as extreme as in some other places in South Wales, and did not manifest itself in an anti-Irish riot or indeed, anything approaching that. Most of the violence involving the Irish in Swansea usually took the form of fights between themselves. There are many items in the *Cambrian* from about 1845 onwards relating to Irish disturbances, many of which were quite humorous. One such case involved a witness in the Bowling Murder Trial. The *Cambrian* of 17 May 1845, reporting on Swansea Petty Sessions, recounted that Timothy Leary (one of the principal witnesses in the trial for John Bowling) and his wife were charged with very disorderly conduct while in a state of intoxication and assaulting the police. They were discharged after being cautioned. Shortly afterwards, the *Cambrian* of 7 June 1845 carried this report:

> S.P.S. - An Irishman applied for a warrant against four of his countrymen who had violently assaulted him. Granted.
>
> **An Irish Row**
> Daniel Bryant, Daniel Sullivan, and James Sullivan were charged with having violently assaulted Timothy Donovan. By the complainant's statement, it appeared that about 9 o'clock on Sunday evening, the parties who were all natives of the Green Island, were near that part of our town at Greenhill assigned for their habitation (and known by the appelation of 'Little Ireland'), when the complainant observed a man named Cornelius Leary strike his sister-in-law, the [complainant] remonstrated with him, on which he received a blow in the face. He had barely had time to return the blow, when Bryant held his arms, and the other defendants joined in assaulting him. They got him upon the ground, when Sullivan and the other defendants kicked him until the ground was deluged with his blood; so violent did they attack him, that he 'really thought he was dead'. (The complainant exhibited the clothes worn at the time which were covered with blood) - John Owen, Smith, an active parish constable, who was called to the spot, deposed to the violence of the attack by the parties, some of whom held the complainant's hands behind him, while the others attached him in front. He could not identify any of the defendants owing to the darkness of the evening. - The defendants called Mary Leary, who swore that the complainant was the first aggressor, having struck Bryant in the first instance. She however, spoke too much, going so far as to state that the complainant was not kicked or beat at all. Defendants were convicted in the penalty of 14/- each, including costs, or one month's imprisonment.

Another typical report concerns Arthur Quinlan in the *Cambrian* of Friday, 29 October 1847.

> **The Navvies again**
> Arthur Quinlan was charged by P.C. Thomas Jones with riotous conduct on Greenhill, on Sunday morning last. The defendant was leader of a gang found

parading the street with bludgeons, and throwing huge stones into the houses as they passed along, to the great terror of the neighbourhood. When the officer came up, the defendant aimed a blow at his head, but missing his aim the policeman sprung upon him and secured him. Fined 5/-, or be imprisoned for 2 months.

Stories such as these become commonplace from the end of the 1840s, owing to the greater numbers of Irish coming into Greenhill, or 'Little Ireland' as it was often termed in the newspapers of the day. The reason for the greater numbers of Irish in Swansea, as elsewhere, was obviously the exodus from Ireland owing to the famine. It is interesting to read the reports of the famine in the *Cambrian* of 12 February 1847:

Editorial: Distress in Ireland - We are happy to learn that so many of the ladies of Swansea are acting on the suggestions embodied in the remarks which appeared in our paper a fortnight since - in exerting themselves with so much zeal and energy in making up coarse clothing to enable the perishing thousands in the Sister Isle to protect themselves from the severity and inclemency of the winter.[5] Misses Nicholl of Cambrian Place have done much.

The editorial continued by condemning Swansea for not making a greater effort:

. . . Swansea, although claiming to be the metropolis of Wales, it has been more backward in the aid it has rendered than many towns half its size and not indebted by way of trade to the extent of one-fourth Swansea is to the sister isle.

It concluded by remarking that Cardiff, Merthyr, and Newport had had their own town meetings to discuss aid for the famine victims.

However, by the end of the month, there had been some improvements. For instance, the *Cambrian* of 26 February 1847 reported on a Concert in Aid of distressed, destitute Irish and Scots, which had been held on Monday, 22 February, under the patronage of the Mayor. This amateur Concert was held at the Assembly Rooms, and was well attended, even though the quality of some of the acts was truly 'amateur'. The following is an example of the 'poetry' that was heard:

Oh! list to the cry that from Erin's sad isle
Thrills each heart with a sympathy deep;
For sorrow hath darkened the light of its smiles
and many a mourner doth weep.

by L.N. of Swansea (written expressly for the occasion) (Sung by Mrs Farndell)

Sympathy for famine victims in Ireland contrasted sharply with sentiments felt towards the local Irish. The *Cambrian* of 23 April 1847, a mere two months after the concert, printed this

Report on the Irish in Swansea/Greenhill:

Vagrancy - the number of Irish vagrants, by whom this town and neighbourhood are infested, has become a source of great annoyance to the inhabitants, and has contributed to create a considerable increase in the demands of the poor rate. The melancholy tales, impoverished appearance and supplicating attitudes of some of these persevering and sturdy beggars present a strange contrast to the schemes occasionally witnessed by those who, in the execution of their duties, are called upon to visit the lodging houses in the vagrant Irish colony localised at Greenhill in this town. Two active officers of our police force, who had occasion last week to inspect a portion of the district in question were astonished at the revelry and good living in which the inhabitants flourished. Amidst the greatest filth and uncivilization, there was in almost every house a profusion of roast and boiled beef, pork, mutton, and every description of meat, and abundance of peas and other vegetables; in fact greater quantities of all eatables than would be found in the dwelling-houses of the best paid mechanics in what is generally termed 'the lower town'. There were likewise card playing and other amusements carried on in nearly every house. Such scenes were not only observable in the houses of those who earn good wages in the copper and other works, while they send their wives with their own and borrowed children about the town and country to beg, but even amongst the very lowest classes - those who subsist entirely by begging, etc., the 'nothing-to-eat- since- yesterday-morning' men, who sometimes so successfully practise on the credulity of good ladies and gentlemen. We doubt not that a good deal of distress prevails amongst the poorer classes, but it is equally certain that much imposition and fraud on the benevolent public are likewise carried on.

Many of the Irish who came to the South Wales ports were brought over illegally by masters of ships for a small payment, or even free, as they were the most convenient form of ballast for the ship, owing to the fact that they could board and disembark of their own free will! During the 1840s, there were many reports of these illegal Irish immigrants.[6] The *Cambrian* of 28 March 1851 reported one of the earliest such landings in the vicinity of Swansea:

Caution to Masters of Vessels. We understand that a master of a vessel landed a party of Irish at the Mumbles this week, having brought them over from the coast of Ireland for 2s each. They arrived in Swansea in a state of great destitution, and immediately applied for relief to the Relieving Officer. Having ascertained who the master of the vessel was, an application was made by Mr Daniel for a summons against him, which was granted on Wednesday. This is the first importation by sea of this somewhat plentiful Irish commodity we have had at Swansea, and we trust if the captain is proved to be guilty of such an offence, he will, whoever he may be, be visited with the utmost rigour the law

Plate 6: Pont y Glasdwr and Llangyfelach Road from Dyfatty.

June, 1989.

Plate 7: Llangyfelach Road showing R. C. School, Cathedral, and 'The Brynmelyn' Public House.

allows, and thus taught he is not to inundate us with such hungry customers with impunity. We hope also the Coast Guard, whose duty it is to prevent such landing, will keep a sharper look out for the future.

Other news items, such as this story in the *Cambrian* of 12 January 1855, refer to the removal of the destitute Irish, and their lack of cooperation!

Irish Paupers:-

At our Petty Sessions, on Tuesday last, Mr. Daniel, the relieving officer of the Swansea Union, applied to the Bench for the necessary order to transport no less than twelve Irish paupers, including their children, to their native parishes in Ireland. Incredible as it may appear, it is nevertheless a fact, that the indoor support, and out-door relief given to these Irish paupers amount to no less a sum than £800 or £1,000 per annum, and hence the necessity which exists of relieving our parishes of such encumbrances by forwarding them to their native isle. Many of these paupers show the greatest obstinacy in answering the necessary questions - preferring the accommodation afforded them at the Union to the somewhat precarious chances of subsistence in their native parish.

Swansea Petty Sessions - Irish Stubbornness:-

Several orders were made for the removal of paupers to their own parishes. One woman of true Milesian blood, named Catherine Shea, positively refused to make the necessary statement as to her native place. The folowing colloquy ensued:
Clerk: Take the book in your right hand.
Shea: I shan't take the book at all.
Clerk: You cannot make the statement without the oath.
Shea: I don't care, I'll not take the book. I can't swear to the truth.
Clerk: If you don't take the book you will be sent to gaol.
Shea: Send me then - I don't care.

. . . evidently she did not want to go back to the 'ould counthry'. She begged to be sent to Merthyr, saying that she should there soon hear from her husband who was in 'Ameriky'. It transpired that she was born in Kerry, Ireland.

The local press also provides a graphic insight into living conditions in Greenhill at the time. For instance, an interesting and informative series of articles appeared in the *Cambrian* in the course of 1853, under the titles 'A Visit to the Courts and Alleys of Swansea' and 'A Visit to the Common Lodging Houses of Swansea'.

A visit to the Courts and Alleys of Swansea . . .

This week it is our intention to conduct the reader a little higher up the town, and request him to enter with us into one or two of the vagrant lodging-houses which are to be found in the neighbourhood of Greenhill.

After our peregrinations through Howell's court our guide conducted us in

Swansea Local Board of Health 1852. Survey of the Borough of Swansea

SCALE, 44 FEET TO AN INCH.

Map 8: Detail from Swansea Local Board of Health, 1852.

the first place to no. 44, Back Street. The landlady of this house, ever mindful of 'turning a penny' had placed very conspicuously in her window a card announcing in most polite terms 'that travellers could be accommodated with beds, etc.' We accordingly entered, but soon found that the outside (which was anything but tempting was indeed far preferable to the inside. Crouched before a small fire, and in perfect darkness, we found the landlord, a true son of the Emerald Isle, freely indulging in 'blowing a cloud', whilst his better-half and some six or eight lodgers were engaged in a most animated, but not very edifying discussion over a cup of tea. This room seemed to serve for almost every purpose - in one corner was piled a huge heap of rags and bones, evidently the proceeds of the perambulatings of the day. We found the house in a most disgraceful state - the ground had not apparently been cleansed for a month - dirt and filth literally covered the floor; the walls were filthy in the extreme, whilst the whole habitation bespoke the negligence and dirty habits of the occupants. Having obtained a light, we succeeded, after great exertions, in gaining an entrance to the second storey, which we found in the same wretched condition; as many as ten were sleeping on the ground of this room. We next directed our steps to the house of Mrs. Sullivan, of Greenhill Street, which on entering, we found neatly kept, but very crowded with lodgers. A large room at the back of this house has been fitted up with every convenience as a workshop for pedlars.[7]

The story continued on 8 April:

A visit to the courts and alleys of Swansea . . .

. . . On Wednesday evening last 6 April 1853 we again sallied forth on a visit to some few more of those haunts of poverty and vice which abound in various parts of our town.

In some houses could be seen clusters of young boys, and a number of girls of from 15 to 17 years of age, who, bereft of all modesty and female delicacy, frequently mingled in a giddy dance, whilst the 'fiddler' sent forth 'sweet notes' from his skilfully-played instrument. In other houses, a 'motley group' were seated round a small fire, listening most attentively to the song of some favoured mistress, who in the most hearty manner, called upon her friends to join in chorus; and then would the whole house vibrate with the song of these wretched beings; and thus it was 'they passed away a merry tune, unchecked by cares or woe'.

Although, then, these individuals are compelled to endure the greatest privations and although they are plunged in the deepest degradation and wretchedness we yet see among them such familiarity, such good feeling existing, such hilarity of spirits, such freedom from anxiety and care, that we imagine they are recompensed in a great measure for all their privations and wants.[8]

This account is particularly interesting because it attests to the indomitable spirit of the Irish people who had to endure living in such conditions as these, and also to the fact that they brought with them their Irish musical traditions and culture.

This last item from the *Cambrian* of 23 September 1853, echoes the *Health Reports* which were the subject of Chapter III.

Editorial - The Cholera . . .
. . . can we not, with as much certainty as though the cases had already occurred, point out the courts and alleys, the bye-streets, and even, in many cases, the houses where cholera will first show itself and where safely domiciled, it will continue as long as the epidemic influence remain? Is it not in the crowded, filthy, and ill-ventilated abodes of the Irish at Greenhill, in the hovels of Howells Court, or the filthy purlieus of Jockey Street and John Street, that we may fairly look for its approach and expect to herald its advent amongst us?

This dire picture was further reflected in the lodgings to be found in Greenhill.

A Visit to the Common Lodging Houses of Swansea:

Mitchell's Row:- In this row, situated in the far-famed locality of 'Little Ireland', are to be found three or four notorious vagrant lodging houses, all in the most filthy and wretched state. The rapacious landlady of one, Margaret Shean, a native of the 'Emerald Isle', had safely housed, in two very circumscribed dirty appartments, no less than 13 lodgers, although she most positively assured us, before our entrance, that she had none but her own 'childhrin'. This number was composed principally of men and women, who had taken up their abode for the night on some straw strewed on the floor.

In the domicile of Humphrey Driscoll, in the same row we found no less than 16 human beings packed together in a small room, which appartment was in the most filthy state, and should immediately be cleansed and white-washed.

In John Kelly's house in the same row, we found only a few lodgers, but the house was in a truly lamentable condition - the floor being covered with bones, dirty rags, junk and other nuisances.

Several other lodging-houses in Emma Street, and Charles Street, were next visited.
. . . we would request the Town Council at their meeting today to not only have the proper cleaning and repairs of the streets in this locality, but also for the purpose of preventing vagrant lodging houses being nightly infested with such numbers of the worst description of characters, whose filthy and extremely dirty habits, even in the houses, are quite likely to induce and engender disease in its most virulent form as the deposit of rubbish and ashes in the court.[9]

The Greenhill area, which was the main home for the Irish in Swansea during the nineteenth century, has been described both in local folklore and in scholarly studies as one of the most socially deprived areas of the town. From contemporary written accounts, it has to be accepted that this grim idea was in fact, a reality.

Nevertheless, this 'bleak and bare hillside' was the refuge for many generations of Irish immigrants, and developed a character which was undeniably unique within Swansea.

NOTES

1. The *Cambrian*, 31 March 1804.
2. The *Cambrian*, 17 May 1834.
3. The National Library of Wales, Calendar of the Diary of Lewis Weston Dillwyn, Vol. ii, 18 November 1823 - 31 December 1833.
4. The *Swansea Journal*, 8 March 1843.
5. The Reports of the Commissioners of Inquiry into the State of Education in Wales, p.375, bear this out by the statement, 'Free School, York Place (Girls' School). I found all the elder part of this school busily engaged in making clothes for the destitute Irish'.
6. C. Woodham-Smith, *The Great Hunger*, p.280.
7. The *Cambrian*, 4 March 1853.
8. The *Cambrian*, 8 April 1853.
9. The *Cambrian*, 23 September 1853.

Chapter Five

The Surnames of the Swansea Irish and their places of origin in Ireland

In this chapter, surnames extracted from the written evidence on the earliest Irish settlers in Swansea are examined, and compared with those places in Ireland where they are most prevalent[1],

Appendix I contains a list of Irish individuals and families which appear in the Census Enumerators' Returns of 1841, 1851 and 1861. It is likely that the material on the Irish from the 1841 Census is more comprehensive than that from the later censuses, as the Irish population of Swansea was, of course, much smaller at that time. For the censuses of 1851 and 1861, the author deliberately concentrated on the Irish living in the locality of Greenhill and neighbouring districts. But before turning to the census material it should be borne in mind that Swansea is fortunate in having additional demographic evidence for the nineteenth century, which predates the first useful national census of 1841.

Two surveys of the Town and Franchise of Swansea were carried out by the Statistical Society of the Royal Institution of South Wales. The first was in 1837 and was credited to a George Jones, and the other was in October 1839. They were, in effect, a sort of local census. They listed the names of house occupiers, and, while not giving their full address, did give the name of the street. In spite of the fact that they only listed the name of the head of the household and not the names of the members of his family, they are still a useful source of evidence for early Irish settlement in Swansea in the decade preceding the Irish famine. The survey of October 1839, more importantly, in terms of this study, has a column under the heading 'Native of', giving the place of origin of each informant. This survey also lists the 'Religious Principles' of each person. For the purpose of this study all the information on the Irish inhabitants of Swansea, according to both surveys has been extracted and included below.

Firstly, the material from the Survey of the Town and Franchise of Swansea by George Jones 1837:

Occupier	*Proprietor*
Frog Street	
Mr John Sullivan	Mr Rees
Park Street	
Jno. H. Hogan	Mrs Sophie Richards
Edward Terrace/Rutland Place	
Mr Edward Murphy	Edward Murphy
Princess Street	
? Fitzgerald	Rich.Richards
Greenhill and *Court behind*	
No Irish names	
Ebenezer Street or *Ann Street*	
Saml. Melon	Saml. Melon
Bargemans Row	
Andrew Driscoll	T. Gibbs
Bedford Row or *Jockey Street*	
Cathrine Hanlon	R. Richards
Queen Street	
Wm. McCarthy	Ann Bowen
Back Lane	
Thomas Quin	Howell Hopkins
Waun Wen	
Timothy Moran	David Jones
near Coppermans Arms	
Ann Redmond	Ann Redmond
Miles Sweeny	Evan Lewis
Charles Street	
Timothy Coghlan	Wm. Williams (near 'Globe')
Thomas Lynch	Wm. Williams
Thomas Casey	David Philips
Bath. Sullivan	- Richardson
Jno. O'Brien	- Richardson

Dinis Mullins	Wm. Beddoe (near 'Ivy Bush')
Back of the Woollen Factory, a continuation of Greenhill	
Mary Hagon	Wm. Griffiths
Melville Street	
Amy Royley	Mrs Cathrine Jenkins
Mr Job Sullivan	Mrs Cathrine Jenkins
Welcome to Town Lane	
Rd. Redmond	Da. Daniels
Mount Pleasant	
Thomas O'Neil	T. Powell

Of this total of twenty-three names, it is interesting to note that there was a conspicuous absence of Irish names in Greenhill Street. However, already, at this period, six Irish people were listed as inhabiting Charles Street.

The second Survey of October 1839 is an interesting and useful source because it actually gives the place of origin of each individual, together with their religion, and occupation.

Name of Occupant			*Native of*	*Religious Principles*
Hugh Mahony	44 Poppit Hill *Waun Wen*		Maulnih Muck	Church of Rome
Timothy Liany	169	Labourer	Bearheevan	C of R
Larrence Meany	186	Labourer	Clonmel	C of R
Cornelious Hurley	204	Labourer	Timilage	C of R
Jn. Donovan	218	Tinman	Rass Carling	C of R
W. Walsh	221	Shoemaker	Kerry	C of R
Michael Keasy	223	Labourer	Co. Limerick	C of R
Patrick Sullivan	229	Labourer	Co. Cork	C of R
M. Sweeney	232	Labourer	near Bandon	C of R
William Feagan	234	Labourer	White Haven	C of R
Thos. Keasy		Labour	Cove of Cork	C of R
John Mahony		Labour	near Cork	C of R
Jno. Murphy		Labourer	C. of Cork	C of R
James Canly		Labourer	Castle Townsend, Co. Cork	C of E
Daniel M. Wallenin		Labourer	near Cork	C of R
Samuel Ford		Shoemaker	near Bandon, Co. Cork	C of R
Jeremiah O'Neil		Labourer	Castle Townsend, Co. Cork	C of R
Timuthy Myrane		Labourer	near Clahnikilty, Co. Cork	C of R

Name of Occupant		*Native of*	*Religious Principles*
Patrick Purchil	Labourer	near Cork	C of R
James Sullivan	Labourer	Clahnikilty	C of R
Patrick Murray	Smith	Turlo, Co. of Meeo	C of R
Margaret Lynch	Labourer	Wexford	C of R
James Murray	Smith	Meeo	C of R
Richard Keatin	Labourer	Tiperary	C of R
Jn. Corcorane	Labourer	Clohnikilty, Co. Cork	C of R
Jas. Neals	Weaver	Clohnikilty, Co. Cork	C of R
Patrick Ryan	Shoemaker	Limberick	C of R
Jerimiah Sullivan	Labourer	Timilage, Co. of Cork	C of R
James Walsh	Tanner (Morriston)	Dublin	C of R
Larrance Lynch	Labourer	Co. Limberick	C of E
Andrew Driskel	Labourer	Skeberine	C of R

This survey concludes with the note 'Keeper of Book for 1840s: Hugh Mahony.' Mahony was the caretaker of the Royal Institution of South Wales at this time.

Altogether there are thirty-one Irish people listed in this survey. Of those, nineteen were from County Cork, and seven of the others from neighbouring counties.

Plate 8: Casey Roofing Lorry, Pont y Glasdwr, Greenhill, June 1989.

The evidence of the 1830s surveys is amplified by the records of St David's Priory, and, in particular, the Register of Baptisms. During the incumbency of Revd James Fleetwood, 1824 to 1829 the following names were entered:

1824 bap. of Anna Power d. of Thomas and Mary Anne Power (of Neath)
bap. of Michael Bourke son of Michael Bourke and Joan Sullivan
bap. of John Sullivan son of ? and Margaret Murphy
1826 bap. of John Casey son of Peter Casey and Anna Power (Clonikily)
1827 bap. of Maria Driskill d. of ? and Catharine Driskill of Co. Cork
1818 bap. of Daniel Connell son of Patrick Connel and Catharine McCarthy

From 1831 to 1832 the church of St David's was served by Revd Robert Platt, and during these years he baptised the following eight Irish children:

16/02/1831 bap. of Mary d. of Timothy Coughlan and Johane
29/06/1831 bap. of John son of John McDonnell and Bridgit
April 1831 bap. of Jeremiah son of Patrick O'Connel and Catherine
23/02/1832 bap. of Michael son of Andrew Driskill and Mary
01/04/1832 bap. of Dennis son of Jeremiah Neil and Catharine
01/04/1832 bap. of John son of Cornelius Ryan and Margaret
17/02/1832 bap. of John son of Daniel Coughlin and Anora
04/11/1832 bap. of John son of Jeremiah Driskill and Catherine

The St David's Priory Index of Baptisms, enables one to ascertain the names of the earliest Irish families recorded in Swansea. Well before the great influx of Irish in the wake of the famine of the late 1840s, the following names occur:

1809 Driscoll.
1811 Brenan; O'Brien.
1812 Finigan.
1813 Cutery; Noonan: Scanlon.
1814-24 No resident priest.
1820 Scully.
1824 Bourke; Power; Sullivan.
1825 Connell; Flood; Hanlon; Sleatery.
1826 Casey; Corolin; Gilakin; Landragan.
1827 Danganay; Driskill; Hagarty; Keane.
1828 Coughlan; Fitzgerald; Mahony; McDonnell; McNamara; Walsh.
1829 Farrel; Mullins; O'Neill; Purcell.

1830	Donohoe; Hearn; Keilly; Lehane; Murphy; Neal: Nugent; Regan; Slattery.
1831	Dorsey; O'Connell.
1832	Aherne; Clancy; Collins; Corsey; Riley; Ryan; Scandlin.
1833	Corty; Larkin; Stack.
1834	Begley; Corkoran; Cotter; Cullen; de Courcy.
1835	Kenny; Maher; Sweeney; Welch.
1836	Cleary; Connelly; Cronnaly; Dailey; Doyle; Fegan; Maloney.
1837	Cronin; Leary; Welsh.
1838	Dunavon; Halloran.
1839	Dower; Kealan; Sexton; Trenor; Wall.
1840	Bolland; Cahill; Cogly; Conor; Crowly; Hurley; Kealy; Keogh; Linahan; Mainey; Mara; Ponsonby.

According to one authority on the distribution of Irish surnames,[2] the twenty-six most common surnames in the County Cork are as follows: 1. O'Sullivan/Sullivan; 2. Murphy; 3. McCarthy; 4. O'Mahony/Mahony; 5. O'Donavon/Donavon; 6. Walsh; 7. O'Brien; 8. O'Callaghan/Callaghan; 9. O'Leary/Leary; 10. Crowley; 11. Collins; 12. O'Driscoll/Driscoll; 13. O'Connell/Connell; 14. Barry; 15. Cronin; 16. Buckley; 17. Baly; 18. Sheehy; 19. O'Riordan/Reardon; 20. Kelleher; 21, O'Connor/Connor; 22. Hurly; 23. Regan; 24. O'Keefe/Keefe; 25. Harrington; 26. Fitzgerald. Eighteen of these names are recorded in the above Baptismal Index of St David's Priory, and all of them are to be found in the succeeding years.

Many of the above-mentioned surnames are also common in neighbouring counties, but each of those counties also have their own distinctive names, which are also found among the Irish immigrants into Swansea in the nineteenth century. For instance O'Shea/Shea, is the third most common name in County Kerry, Brosnan is the tenth, followed by Foley, with Lynch in fifteenth place. The distinctive names of County Clare include McNamara, which is the second most common, followed by Moloney, with Halloran/O'Halloran and Clancy at tenth, eleventh and thirteenth, respectively. The commonest surname in County Limerick is Ryan, as well as in County Tipperary, where it is three times more common than the next three strongest surnames, which are Maher, O'Brien and Kennedy. The remaining county of Munster, County Waterford, has Power and Walsh, as the first and second most common surnames.

The counties of Leinster province also have their distinctive

Plate 9: McNamara's Electrical Shop, Dillwyn Street, June 1989.

surnames. County Wexford, as has been mentioned elsewhere in this study, has many names which derive from the alien invaders who settled there from the twelfth century onwards[3]. These non-Gaelic names include, Roche, Rossiter, Codd, Stafford, Synott/Sinnott, Hore, Talbot and Devereux. Murphy is the most common native Irish name, followed by Doyle and thirdly, Walsh, followed by O'Byrne, Cullen and Kavanagh. County Carlow shares many of these names, including Nolan and Whelan. Kilkenny has a similar spread of names, and also, Brennan/O'Brennan, being the most common surname in this county. One could go on by listing the names of the remaining counties of Leinster, including Dublin, but we would be moving away from the counties of the southern seaboard of Ireland. All the evidence shows that it was from these counties that the mass of the immigrants into Swansea came from, as well as those Irish who settled in the rest of South Wales and Bristol.

We can now turn to the evidence supplied by the census. Unfortunately, the 1841 census does not give specific details of the place of origin of individuals. But the capital letter 'I' is normally placed in the 'where born' column for Irish persons. Of the Irish settled in Swansea according to the 1841 census, the most common surname by far is Sullivan, with about sixty examples. There are

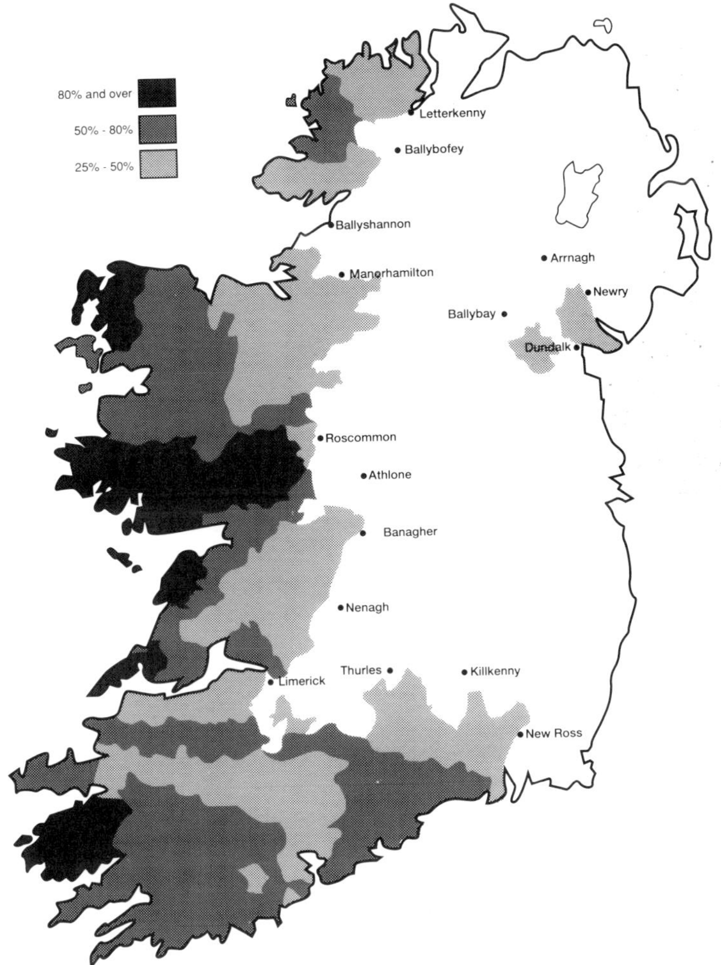

Map 9: Linguistic Map of Ireland showing the distribution of Irish speakers as shown in the 1851 Census of Ireland.

almost twenty Lynchs and Caseys, a dozen Driscoles and Barrys, followed by McCarthy, Mahony, O'Brien and Corcoran. The surnames Coughlin and Cronin were also prominent.

From the evidence of surname distribution in Ireland, the south-western provenance of the majority of these surnames is plain. In the censuses of 1851 and 1861, there is often a specific reference to the county, or even the town or village from which the Irish immigrants came. It has therefore been possible to extract the relevant details from the census lists of 1851 and 1861 shown in the Appendices, and to tabulate them as follows:

Place of Birth	*1851 Census*	*1861 Census*
Ireland	473	778
Cork	203	135
Kerry	36	30
Waterford	21	38
Tipperary	19	7
Limerick	8	2
Clare	3	2
Total for Munster	**290**	**214**
Leinster	22	10
Ulster	23	3
Connaught	13	3
Swansea	284	529

The above statistics confirm overwhelmingly the preponderance of immigrants from County Cork, followed by the other counties of the Province of Munster, and much smaller numbers from the three other provinces. The totals for the Swansea-born refer to Irish people already established in the town, and to the children of recent immigrants.

Map 9 illustrates the distribution of Irish Gaelic speakers in Ireland according to the census of Ireland for 1851. It will be seen that the Province of Munster had substantial areas which were fifty to eighty per cent Gaelic at this time, including most of the coastal belt, parts of Kerry and Clare had over eight per cent Gaelic, and even the hinterland of Cork City show twenty-five to fifty per cent levels of Gaelic. However, it is virtually impossible to estimate the number of

Irish immigrants into Swansea in the middle of the nineteenth century who were able to speak Irish Gaelic, but the evidence supplied in Map 9 makes it probable that there was a certain number who could.

Although twentieth-century slum clearance in the Greenhill area has reduced the number of habitations in the part of town traditionally occupied by the Irish, the City of Swansea Register of Electors for 1989 reveals a large number of persons with Irish surnames still living in the area:

Brynmelin Street
Collins, Murphy
Carmarthen Road
Connor, Dower
Cwm Road
Brien, Collins, Daley, Gorman, Lynch, McCarthy, Murphy, O'Connell, O'Kelly, O'Rourke, O'Sullivan, Shannon
Llangyfelach Street
Casey, Conway, Dugon, Kavanagh, McCarthy, Murphy, Sullivan
Pontyglasdwr
Connor, Dower

These Irish surnames are a legacy of the original Irish immigrants, and are prominent in Swansea today (see Plates 8 and 9).

Chapter I began by describing the long and continuous links which exist between south-west Wales and southern Ireland. This study ends with an Irish ballad, which, according to two standard works on Irish traditional ballads, originated in Swansea. The song is called 'The Holy Ground'. O'Lochlainn noted that 'Cork men maintain that 'The Holy Ground' is the waterfront of Cobh (Queenstown), but others hold that it is Swansea dockland,[4] thereby expressing only a possibility. However, the other work by Healy, goes further, and gives the specific information that 'Just as "The Banks" has become the anthem of Cork, "The Holy Ground" has become the anthem of Cobh, the pretty little seaport town of Cork Harbour. It is not originally an Irish song, since it was first heard of in Swansea, in Wales: but it has become so much a part of the scene down South that it cannot be considered out of place in an Irish songbook. There is, in fact, a district in Cobh known as "The Holy Ground" at the eastern end of the town, and it is, or was, the part where most of the sea-going population dwelt; so that the song is most appropriate to its present place of adoption'.[5] Healy adds that both the words and music are Welsh traditional. There are slight variations between the version of the song in his book and in O'Lochlainn's, but these are indicated where they occur below:

The Holy Ground

Adieu my fair young maiden(s), a/ten thousand times adieu,
We must bid goodbye to the Holy Ground, and the place/girls that we love true,
We will sail the salt sea over, and return again for sure, to seek the girls
That/who wait for us - In the Holy Ground once more.
Fine girl you are,
You're/For the girl I do adore, and still I live in Hope(s) to see, The Holy Ground once more - Fine girl you are!
We're on the Salt Sea sailing and you are safe behind

Fond letters I will write to you, the secrets of my mind,
Fond letters I will to you, the girl I do adore
and still I live in hope to see the Holy Ground once more.
Fine girl you are, You're the girl I do adore,
And still I live in hope to see,
The Holy Ground once more - Fine girl you are!

I see a storm arising, I can see it coming soon
For/Oh the night is/was dark and dreary/stormy,
You can scarcely/scarce could see the moon
And the/our good old ship she is tossing about/was tossed about,
And her rigging(s) is all tore/all was torn:
With her seems agape and leaky, with her timbers dozed and old,
But/And still I live(d) in hope(s) to see, The Holy Ground once more,
You're the girl I do adore, and still I live in hope(s) to see,
The Holy Ground once more - Fine girl you are!

And now the storm is over and we are safe on shore
Let us drink/and a health we'll drink to the Holy Ground and the girls (that) we('d) adore:
We will drink strong ale and porter, and/till we make the taproom(s) roar
And when our money is all/all is spent we will go to sea for more.
Fine girl you are, You're the girl I do adore, and still I live in hope(s)
to see, The Holy Ground once more - Fine Girl You Are!

NOTES

1. B. de Breffny, *Irish Family Names* (Dublin, 1982); E. Maclysaght, *The Surnames of Ireland* (Shannon, 1969), *SRSI*, Appendix to Twenty-Ninth Report of the Registrar-General.
2. *Op. cit.*; *IFN*, pp.14-18.
3. D. O'Muirithe, 'The Anglo-Normans and their English Dialect of South-East Wexford', p.37.
4. C. O'Lochlainn, *More Irish Street Ballads*, p.220.
5. *The Second Book of Irish Ballads*, ed. J.N. Healy, p.30.

Appendix I

The Census of 1841

	Age			Where Born
House of Correction				
John Leary	10	Prisoner	-	Ireland
John Ryan	20	Prisoner	Mariner	Ireland
Jeremiah Finn	35	Prisoner	Pedler	Ireland
Jeremiah Molowney	30	Prisoner	Servant	Ireland
Union Workhouse				
Bridget Ians	50	-	-	Ireland
Swansea Infirmary				
Cornelius Sullivan	47		Labourer	Ireland
Swansea Infantry Barracks				
Samuel Kamy	25		Military	Ireland
James Mullen	25		Military	Ireland
William McConochie	35		Military	Ireland
Robert Sudrey	25		Military	Ireland
Patrick Kelly	20		Military	Ireland
Owen Kearnes	35		Military	Ireland
James Dougherty	30		Military	Ireland
Edward Canning	35		Military	Ireland
James Williams	35		Military	Ireland
Thomas Finch	35		Military	Ireland
James O'Brien	35		Military	Ireland
Sketty				
John Burke	20		M.J.	Ireland
Mary Burke	20		-	Ireland
Michael Gahayan	35		Tailor	Ireland
Pentre Guinea				
Mary Clansey	30		Dressmaker	Ireland
Hillfield Cottage				
Honora Sullivan	20		Family Servant	Ireland
Patrick Pursell	40		Labourer	Ireland
Hanah Pursell	35		-	Ireland
John Pursell	9		-	-
Eliza Pursell	3		-	-
Elizabeth Hamilton	11		-	Ireland
Jeffrey Sullivan	35		Ag. Labourer	Ireland
Elen Sullivan	35		-	Ireland
Thomas Sullivan	15		-	Ireland

Mary Sullivan	8	-	Ireland
James Sullivan	5	-	Ireland
John Sullivan	2	-	Ireland
John McCarty	20	-	Ireland
Institution (R.I.S.W.)			
Hugh Mahony	35	Keeper of Institution	Ireland
Elizabeth Mahony	30	Wife of Above	Ireland
Honora Mahony	5	-	-
Eleanor Mahony	4	-	-
Elizabeth Mahony	2	-	-
York Place			
James Mahony	25	Labourer	Ireland
Wind Street			
Edward Forthogirl	25	Shoemaker	Ireland
Daniel O'Connell	25	Coachman	Ireland
Gower Street			
Thomas Johnston	35	Tea dealer	Ireland
Isabella Johnston	3	-	-
Margaret Johnston	1	-	-
Jns. Duggan	15	Tea dealer App.	Ireland
Thos. Brodwick	20	Tea dealer App.	Ireland
Marn. Molowney	15	Tea dealer App.	Ireland
Castle Street			
William Reynalds	35	Porter	Ireland
James Kinny	25	-	Ireland
Timothy Leary	25	-	Ireland
College Street			
Joseph Fox	30	Cord winder	Ireland
Charlotte Fox	30	-	-
Thomas Fox	8	-	-
Mary Fox	7	-	Ireland
William Fox	5	-	-
Ellen Fox	2	-	-
David Bourke	20	Cord winder	Ireland
Orchard Street			
William Kelly	20	Taylor	Ireland
Clifton Terrace			
John Beyan	23	Shipwright App.	Ireland
Pleasant Row			
William Byrne	25	Seaman	Ireland

Oxford Street			
Edward Linch	25	Cattle dealer	Ireland
Eleanor Linch	20	-	Ireland
Thomas Murphy	30	Cattle dealer	Ireland
Patrick Lains	30	Cattle dealer	Ireland
Mary Holland	21	-	Ireland
Park Street			
Martin Hennessy	45	School master	Ireland
Elizabeth Hennessy	45	-	Ireland
Bernard Hennessy	18	-	Ireland
Orange Street			
Jas. Sullivan	35	-	Ireland
Hanah Sullivan	35	-	Ireland
Catharine Sullivan	6	-	-
Mary Brien	35	Female Servant	Ireland
Danl. Reiley	25	Feather? dealer	Ireland
Margaret Reiley	25	-	Ireland
Mary Reiley	6	-	Ireland
Norah Fowley	30	-	Ireland
Mount Pleasant			
Margaret Mahon	60	Independant	Ireland
Michael Miron	15	M.S.	Ireland
Green Dragon Lane			
John Loveless	67	Mariner	Ireland
Cross Street			
Patrick Cummins	38	Hawker	Ireland
Catharine Cummins	40	Hawker	Ireland
William Cummins	10	-	Swansea
Edward Handlin	40	Hawker	Ireland
Charles McCoy	20	Hawker	Ireland
James O'Hagan	35	Hawker	Ireland
Patrick O'Hagan	14	Hawker	Ireland
Frog Street			
Richard Byens	25	Labourer	Ireland
Michael Burke	25	Butcher	Ireland
Ann Burke	25	Dressmaker	-
Timothy Hanagan	25	Excavator	Ireland
Ellen Hanagan	30	-	Ireland
Edward Chard	30	Sailmaker	Ireland
Mary Chard	25	-	-
George Chard	15	App. Shipwright	Ireland
Mathew Chard	8 mths	-	-

Helina Deacy	30	Widow	Ireland
Deborah Deacy	2	-	-
Victoria Place			
Anne Sullivan	35	Dressmaker	Ireland
Anne Sullivan	15	Daughter	Ireland
Margaret Sullivan	20	Daughter	Ireland
Esther Donne	40	Trader	Ireland
William Donne	14	-	-
Mary Donne	11	-	-
Christopher Cummins	35	Bell Hanger	Ireland
Greenfield Row			
Barney Smith	35	Tinner	Ireland
Bridgett Smith	30	-	Ireland
Elizabeth Smith	1	-	-
Garden Street			
David Kinnear	55	Independant	Ireland
Ann Kinnear	30	Independant	Ireland
Mysid Field			
Timothy Lenihan	30	Tanner	Ireland
Princess Street			
Peter Fitzgerald	60	Gardener	Ireland
Peter Fitzgerald	14	-	-
Union Building			
Judith Logan	60	Independant	Ireland
William Glynne	40	Independant	Ireland
Mary Ann Glynne	30	Independant	-
William John Glynne	10	-	Ireland
Susannah Glynne	5	-	-
High Street			
John Smith	25	M.S.	Ireland
Ann Rogers	25	Milliners App.	Ireland
Philip Wilkins	50	Independant	Ireland
John Mackey	20	Hawker	Ireland
Edw. Chasey	25	Bookseller	Ireland
Arthur Rouny	40	Labourer	Ireland
Mary Mack	52	-	Ireland
Eleanor Broham	20	-	Ireland
Catherine Davies	82	-	Ireland
Back Lane			
William White	-	Cordwaner	Ireland
New Street			
John Kelly	-	Lodger	Ireland

Mariners Row (South Side)			
James Walters	55	Shoemaker	Ireland
Michael Walters	25	Shoemaker	Ireland
Ann Walters	25	-	Swansea
Grace Rees	30	Schoolmistress	-
Sarah Martin	20	Assistant S.M.	Ireland
Court in High Street			
Norah Casey	30	Independant	Ireland
Catharine Casey	15	-	-
Michael Delany	21	Labourer	Ireland
Bridget Delaney	17	-	Ireland
Mary Cronin	40	-	Ireland
Thomas Cronin	30	-	Ireland
Mary Cronin	25	-	Ireland
Ann Cronin	2	-	Ireland
Mary Cronin	1	-	Ireland
William Kiff	30	Labourer	Ireland
Thomas Kiff	11	-	Ireland
Michael Kiff	4	-	Ireland
Croft Street			
Timothy Myran	45	Labourer	Ireland
Ellen Myran	40	-	Ireland
Denis Burns	30	Labourer	Ireland
Johanna Burns	20	-	Ireland
Owen Court			
Margaret Green	30	-	Ireland
Denis Mahony	20	Ag. Labourer	Ireland
Andrew Wilson	15	Labourer	Ireland
James Crawford	40	Ag. Labourer	Ireland
Mary Crawford	3	-	Ireland
William Crawford	22	-	Ireland
James Johnson	55	Joiner	Ireland
Elizabeth Johnson	45	-	-
Edward Johnson	20	-	-
Charles Johnson	12	-	-
George Johnson	10	-	-
Henry Johnson	8	-	-
Strand			
James Criddle	30	Coach painter	Ireland
Hariet Criddle	30	-	-
Ellen Criddle	7	-	-
Jno. Criddle	3	-	-

James Criddle	8	-	-
Thos. Koanan	25	Tailor	Ireland
Sarah Koanan	30	-	-
Richard Mathison	43	Cordwainer	Ireland
Daniel Mathison	16	-	Ireland
Thos. Mathison	10	-	Swansea
Richard Mathison	7	-	Swansea
Margaret Mallison	42	-	Ireland
Hanorah Mallison	21	-	Ireland
Anne Mallison	19	-	Ireland
Mary Mallison	13	-	Ireland
Morris Lane			
Wm. Nash	40	Cordwainer	Ireland
Eliphant and Castle Street			
James Galavun	30	Labourer	Ireland
Mary Galavun	25	-	Ireland
Edward Galavun	4	-	Ireland
Edward Murphy	35	Labourer	Ireland
Ellen Murphy	25	-	Ireland
Patrick Murphy	10	Labourer	Ireland
Margaret Murphy	6	-	Ireland
John Murphy	4	-	Ireland
John Haloran	25	Labourer	Ireland
Johanna Haloran	20	-	Ireland
Old Angel			
Dennis Sullivan	60	Labourer	Ireland
Ellin Sullivan	50	-	Ireland
Mary Sullivan	13	-	Ireland
Timothy Sullivan	11	-	Ireland
James Hayes	45	Labourer	Ireland
Mary Hayes	12	-	-
Dennis Hayes	3	-	-
John Sullivan	30	Labourer	Ireland
Joane Sullivan	20	-	Ireland
Emma Street			
Richard Lowland	30	Painter	Ireland
Mary Lowland	40	-	Ireland
Richard Lowland	10	-	Ireland
Daniel Bowlan	9	-	Ireland
Cathrine Bowlan	15	-	Ireland
Susan Bowlan	3	-	Ireland
Danl. Corcoran	50	Labourer	Ireland

Onora Corcoran	40	-	Ireland
Ellan Corcoran	13	-	Swansea
Patrick Corcoran	11	-	Swansea
John Corcoran	9	-	Swansea
Timothy Corcoran	7	-	Swansea
Mary Corcoran	5	-	Swansea
Denis Downy	20	Labourer	Ireland
Jeremiah Sheeken	25	Labourer	Ireland
Mary Sheeken	30	-	Ireland
Jeremiah Sheeken	5	-	Ireland
Joana Sheeken	2	-	Ireland
Catherine Sheeken	6 mths	-	Swansea
Lawrence Barry	45	Labourer	Ireland
Catherine Barry	40	-	Ireland
James Barry	7	-	Ireland
Eliza Barry	5	-	Ireland
Catharine Barry	10	-	Ireland
Hanah Barry	2	-	Ireland
Michael Sullivan	35	-	Ireland
Patrick Ryan	60	Shoemaker	Ireland
Mary Ryan	58	-	Ireland
Timothy Halpin	25	Labourer	Ireland
Hannah Halpin	20	-	Ireland
John Halpin	1	-	Swansea
Kitty Halpin	4	-	Ireland
Timothy Halpin	20	Labourer	Ireland
Onora Halpin	17	-	Ireland
Cath Sullivan	4	-	Ireland
Catherine Driscoll	30	-	Ireland
Jeremiah Sullivan	30	Hawker	Ireland
Mary Sullivan	25	-	Ireland
Jeremiah Sullivan	1	-	Swansea
Mary Sullivan	9	-	Swansea
Hanora Sullivan	3	-	Swansea
Jeremiah Lynch	20	Labourer	Ireland
Jeremiah Lynch	15	Hawker	Ireland
Catherine Lynch	50	-	Ireland
William Lynch	25	Hawker	Ireland
John Dowling	50	Labourer	Ireland
Michael Dowling	12	-	Swansea
Greenhill			
Stephen Dixon	35	Labourer	Ireland

Abby Dixon	35	-	Ireland
Oliver Hackitt	20	Shoemaker	Ireland
Mary Hackitt	25	-	Ireland
William Lowe	30	M.S.	Ireland
John Shannon	30	Labourer	Ireland
Michael Baine	20	Tinman	Ireland
Dennis Lane	50	Labourer	Ireland
Ellen Lane	35	-	Ireland
Anne Lane	2	-	Swansea
Bite Puris	20	-	Ireland
Robert Puris	2 mths	-	Ireland
Thomas O'Callaghan	25	Shoemaker	Ireland
Patrick Irving	25	Shoemaker	Ireland
Betey Irving	25	-	Ireland
Pat Irving	2 mths	-	-
William Irving	2	-	Ireland
Jeremiah Driscole	30	Labourer	Ireland
Mary Driscole	20	-	Ireland
Mary Driscole	3	-	Swansea
Johannah Driscole	2	-	Swansea
Catherine Driscole	1	-	Swansea
Danl. Murphy	20	Labourer	Ireland
Pat McCarthy	24	Labourer	Ireland
Margaret Carthy	35	-	Ireland
Daniel Hart	50	Shoemaker	Ireland
Lawrence Meany	25	Labourer	Ireland
Mary Meany	30	-	Ireland
Dennis Murphy	20	-	Ireland
Catherine Murphy	12	-	Ireland
Ann Murphy	15	-	Ireland
Bridget Murphy	3	-	Swansea
Ellen Murphy	1	-	Swansea
Hanora Loyan	20	-	Ireland
Caroline Loyan	1	-	Swansea
Thos. Lynch	35	-	Ireland
Edmund O'Brien	30	Labourer	Ireland
Bridgit O'Brien	25	-	Ireland
Mary O'Brien	3	-	Swansea
Ellen O'Brien	1	-	Swansea
Ellen Murphy	20	-	Ireland
James McNamara	30	Labourer	Ireland
Jeremiah McNamara	14	Labourer	Swansea

Jeremiah McCarthy	15	Labourer	Ireland
Catherine McCarthy	40	Independant	Ireland
Michael McCarthy	12	Labourer	Ireland
Percy Brien	45	Netmaker	Ireland
Margaret Brien	12	-	-
Mary Brien	8	-	-
James Sullivan	35	Labourer	Ireland
Mary Sullivan	35	-	Ireland
Kitty Sullivan	12	-	Ireland
Mary Sullivan	10	-	Swansea
James Sullivan	8	-	Swansea
John Sullivan	6	-	Swansea
Danl. Sullivan	4	-	Swansea
Ellen Sullivan	1 mth	-	Swansea
Cornelius Erly	30	Labourer	Ireland
Cathrine Erly	25	-	Ireland
Bridget Erly	3	-	Swansea
Denish Erly	1	-	Swansea
Lucy Grice	20	-	Ireland
William Gana	30	Labourer	Ireland
Jeremiah Sillivan	30	Hawker	Ireland
Mary Sillivan	25	-	Ireland
Jeremiah Sillivan	1	-	Swansea
Mary Sillilvan	9	-	Swansea
Hanora Sillivan	3	-	Swansea
Jeremiah Lynch	20	Labourer	Ireland
Jeremiah Lynch	15	Hawker	Ireland
Catherine Lynch	50	-	Ireland
William Woods	25	Hustler	Ireland
Abigail Woods	20	-	–
John Dowling	50	Labourer	Ireland
Michael Dowling	12	-	Swansea
James Woods	1	-	Swansea
Daniel Cody	20	Hobler	Ireland
Jeremiah Jeffrey	30	Hawker	Ireland
Mary Jeffrey	25	-	Ireland
Mary Ann Jeffrey	7	-	Swansea
Catharine Jeffrey	3	-	Swansea
Catharine Jeffrey	50	-	Ireland
Joseph Black	25	Sailor	Ireland
Thomas Brown	30	Sailor	Ireland
John Collins	30	Sailor	Ireland

Elizabeth Collins	30	-	Ireland
James Dagheny	40	Hawker	Ireland
Fransis Gillon	40	Hawker	-
Mary Dagly	7	-	Ireland
Timithy Tenury	35	Labourer	Ireland
Mary Tenury	30	-	Ireland
Cornelius Tenury	9	-	Ireland
John Tenury	9	-	Ireland
Annora Tenury	7	-	Ireland
Timathy Tenury	3	-	Ireland
Patrick Tenury	2	-	Ireland
Catharine Hanton	25	-	Ireland
Michael Casy	40	Copperman	Ireland
Cathrine Casy	30	-	Ireland
Mary Casy	7	-	Swansea
Cathrine Casy	5	-	Swansea
Annora Casy	2	-	Swansea
N.K. Casy	1 day	-	Swansea
Patrick Denis	25	Labourer	Ireland
John Murray	20	Labourer	Ireland
John Hickey	20	Labourer	Ireland
Nicholas Welsh	45	Shoemaker	Ireland
Cathrine Welsh	35	-	Ireland
Sara Welsh	4	-	Swansea
Mary Welsh	-	-	Swansea
Margaret Donal	60	-	Ireland
James Machnie	50	Labourer	Ireland
Michael Machnie	20	Labourer	Ireland
Caepistyll			
Denis Conel	20	Copperman	Ireland
Daniel Conel	15	Miner	Ireland
Mathew Conel	10	-	Ireland
July Conel	40	-	Ireland
Judy Makanty	40	-	Ireland
Elen Makanty	10	-	Ireland
Cathrine Driscoll	30	-	Ireland
Terrey Conely	5	-	Swansea
Nansi Conely	40	-	Ireland
David Greene	30	Labourer	Ireland
Mary Malom	25	-	Ireland
John Ralph	15	Shoemaker	Ireland
John Haines	30	Labourer	Ireland

James Welsh	20	Shoemaker	Ireland
Walter Cartus	30	Miner	Ireland
Patrick Silivan	40	Labourer	Ireland
Margaret Silivan	35	-	Swansea
Jane Silivan	13	-	Swansea
John Silivan	10	-	Swansea
Catharine Silivan	9	-	Swansea
William Silivan	5	-	Swansea
Miles Swiny	35	Hawker	Ireland
Catherine Swiny	30	-	Ireland
Mary Swiny	15	-	Ireland
Catherine Swiny	10	-	Ireland
Bryan Swiney	10	-	-
Bidy Swiny	8	-	Ireland
John Swiny	5	-	Swansea
Elen Swiny	2	-	Swansea
Miles Swiny	9 mths	-	Swansea
Johanna Crowly	60	-	Ireland
Bridget Crowly	15	-	Ireland
Daniel Sulivan	25	Copperman	Ireland
Margaret Sulivan	20	-	Ireland
Johanna Sulivan	1	-	Swansea
Cornelius Sulivan	25	Labourer	Ireland
Daniel Sulivan	25	Copperman	Ireland
John Horonten	20	Labourer	Ireland
Terrence Cummins	50	Labourer	Ireland
Mary Cummins	30	-	Ireland
Anne Butorme	12	-	Ireland
Brynmelin			
David Scandling	46	Labourer	Ireland
Thomas Scandling	12	-	Swansea
Patrick Murphy	25	Labourer	Ireland
Danl. O'Brien	40	Labourer	Ireland
Mary O'Brien	19	-	Ireland
Pentre Mawr			
Maycal Rickit	25	Labourer	Ireland
Charles Street			
Saml. Ford	35	Shoemaker	Ireland
Margaret Ford	30	-	Ireland
Robert Ford	3	-	Swansea
Denis Dimpsy	40	-	Ireland
Cornelius Sillivan	35	Labourer	Ireland

Mary Sillivan	30	-	Ireland
Danl. Sillivan	8	-	Ireland
Caroline Sillivan	5	-	Ireland
Michael Dowsur	30	Labourer	Ireland
Onora Dowsur	30	-	Ireland
John Cockley	30	Labourer	Ireland
Judith Cockley	30	-	Ireland
Pat. Cockley	4	-	Ireland
Thos. Casey	35	Labourer	Ireland
Catherine Casey	10	-	Ireland
Mary Casey	6	-	Ireland
John Casey	8	-	Ireland
Margaret Casey	3	-	Swansea
Catherine Casey	3	-	Swansea
Ann Casey	3	-	Swansea
John Hughes	15	-	Ireland
John Mahony	30	Labourer	Ireland
Onora Mahony	35	-	Ireland
John Murphy	16	-	Ireland
James Grey	22	Labourer	Ireland
Edward Murphy	20	Labourer	Ireland
Daniel Buckly	30	Labourer	Ireland
Denis Mahony	25	Labourer	Ireland
John White	20	Labourer	Ireland
Maurice Wilch	30	Labourer	Ireland
Tim Leahearne	30	Labourer	Ireland
Wilm. Fitzgerald	25	-	Ireland
Abby Buckly	30	-	Ireland
Kitty Buckly	3	-	-
John Buckly	5 mths	-	-
Mary Fitzgerald	20	-	Ireland
Johanna Fitzgerald	7 mths	-	Swansea
Ellen Wilch	25	-	Ireland
Patrick Wilch	6	-	Ireland
James Wilch	3	-	Ireland
Ellen Wilch	20	-	Ireland
"Ivy Bush" Lewis Griffiths	50	-	Swansea
John Murphy	30	Labourer	Ireland
Onora Murphy	20	-	Ireland
Willm. Murphy	1	-	Swansea
Donl. Cleine	30	Labourer	Ireland
Ellen Cleine	20	-	Ireland

John Keef	60	Labourer	Ireland
John Leary	30	Labourer	Ireland
Catherine Leary	25	-	Ireland
John Leary	2	-	Swansea
Joana Keef	20	-	Ireland
Cornelius Keef	20	Sailor	Ireland
John Keef	15	Butcher	Ireland
Mich. Curtaine	25	Labourer	Ireland
John Corsey	14	Labourer	Ireland
Ellen Corsey	30	-	Ireland
James Corsey	2	-	Ireland
James Carty	35	Labourer	Ireland
Margaret Carty	35	-	Ireland
Ellen Carty	16	-	Ireland
Catherine Carty	19	-	Ireland
Patrick Murray	20	-	Ireland
Danl. Hanolan	30	Copperman	Ireland
Elizabeth Hanolan	25	-	Ireland
Cathrine Hanolan	6	-	Ireland
Timothy Hanolan	3	-	Swansea
Danliel Darky	30	Labourer	Ireland
John Darky	25	-	Ireland
Danliel Darky	5	-	Ireland
Joseph Knowles	30	Weaver	Ireland
Margaret Knowles	40	-	Ireland
Joseph Knowles	6	-	-
John Knowles	3	-	Swansea
Bridgit Knowles	1	-	Swansea
Cornelius Crann	30	-	-
Cornelius Leary	30	Labourer	Ireland
Mary Leary	25	Labourer	Ireland
Michael Leary	6	-	Ireland
Timothy Leary	3	-	Ireland
Mary Leary	1	-	Swansea
William Driskile	25	Labourer	Ireland
Bart. Driskile	15	Labourer	Ireland
Bartholamew Birk	40	Labourer	Ireland
Jeremiah Neal	35	Hawker	Ireland
Catharine Neal	25	-	Ireland
Ellen Neal	15	-	-
Mary Neal	13	-	-
Denis Neal	10	-	Swansea

Patrick Neal	9	-	Swansea
Jeremiah Neal	3	-	Swansea
John Neal	5 mths	-	Swansea
Jeremiah Dempsey	30	-	Ireland
Margaret Dempsey	30	-	Ireland
Peggy Dempsey	10	-	-
Mary Dempsey	7	-	-
Ellen Dempsey	2	-	-
Charles Dempsey	4	-	-
John Bothermoor	40	Hawker	Ireland
Catherine Bothermoor	35	-	Ireland
Sarah Bothermoor	20	-	Ireland
Onora Bothermoor	15	-	Ireland
Fanny Bothermoor	10	-	Ireland
Anna Bothermoor	12	-	Ireland
Catherine Bothermoor	5	-	Ireland
Owen Fisher	40	Hawker	Ireland
Mary Fisher	35	-	Ireland
Margaret Fisher	6	-	Swansea
William Flahavan	35	Copperman	Ireland
William Connor	20	Tailor	Ireland
Edward Keating	20	Shoemaker	Ireland
Ann Keating	20	Dressmaker	Ireland
Elizabeth Keating	1	-	Swansea
William Ponsonby	25	Labourer	Ireland
Margaret Ponsonby	20	Female Servant	Ireland
Catharine Ponsonby	9 mths	-	Swansea
Thos. Enright	25	Labourer	Ireland
Mary Enright	20	-	Ireland
Ellen Enright	2 mths	-	Swansea
Ann Wilson	35	-	Ireland
Mary Wilson	1	-	Swansea
Thos. Wilson	10	-	Swansea
John Wilson	8	-	Swansea
Patrick Wilson	6	-	Swansea
Roger Sheen	20	Copperman	Ireland
Jerh. McCanly	20	Copperman	Ireland
Margaret Lynch	35	-	Ireland
James Murray	45	Wire Worker	Ireland
Ann Murray	45	-	Ireland
Simon Murray	12	-	-
James Murray	10	-	-

Mary Murray	8	-	Swansea
Cathrine Murray	6	-	Swansea
William Walker	30	Labourer	Ireland
William Keating	70	Labourer	Ireland
Richard Keating	20	Labourer	Ireland
Betsy Keating	15	-	Ireland
John Keating	1	-	Swansea
Eugene Carthy	35	Labourer	Ireland
Thos. Hanigen	40	Labourer	Ireland
John Roayther	20	Labourer	Ireland
Edward Collins	25	Labourer	Ireland
John Roche	25	Labourer	Ireland
Mary Roche	25	-	Ireland
Edward Mockler	25	Blacksmith	Ireland
Ann Mockler	25	-	Ireland
Thomas Garman	70	Labourer	Ireland
Ellin Garman	50	-	Ireland
Kitty Garman	11	-	Ireland
Dennis Kinly	23	-	Ireland
Mary Kinly	20	-	Ireland
Timothy Coughlin	40	Labourer	Ireland
Denis Coughlin	18	-	Ireland
John Coughlin	13	-	Swansea
Johanna Coughlin	40	-	Ireland
Mary Coughlin	10	-	Swansea
Catharine Hogan	20	-	Ireland
Henry Sheen	1	-	-

Appendix 2

The Census of 1851

			Age		*Where Born*
Goat Street					
20	Thomas Clancy	Head	49	Servant	Ireland
	Anne Clancy	Wife	43	-	Haverfordwest
	Richard Clancy	Son	6	-	Swansea
Waterloo Street					
	Patrick Cashman	Head	26	Draper & Tea Dealer	Ireland
	Timothy Ledden	Nephew	17	Tea Dealer's Assistant	Ireland
	Bartholomew Whelan	Asst.	20	Travelling Draper	Ireland
	George French	-	25	Comedian	Ireland
Gower Street					
	Martin Cenelly	Head	36	Soldier	Ireland
	Mary Cenelly	Wife	38	-	Ireland
	Mary Mahony	Dame	6	-	Ireland
Dynevor Place					
8	Margaret Maxwell	Dame	17	-	Dublin
	Nicholas Maxwell	Son	12	Scholar	Swansea
	Nancy Ryan	Widow	72	Family Nurse	Limerick
	Sarah Johnson	-	21	Servant	Cork
Castle Bailey					
22	Jane Earley	-	-	Miliners Assistant	Omagh
	Ann Diamond	-	29	Miliners Assistant	Cork
Beaufort Coffee House					
	Elizabeth Sullivan	-	42	Coffee House Keeper	Swansea
	Harriet Sullivan	Daughter	14	Barmaid	Swansea
	+ 3 children	-	5 - 12	Scholars	Swansea
	Johanna McCauliff	-	16	Servant (general)	Ireland
	John Collins	Lodger	35	Ordnance Surveyor	Ireland
Temple Street					
	Wiliam Henry Smith	-	24	Barrister at Law	Ireland
King Street					
9	Charles Scully	Lodger	22	Shoemaker	Co. Cork
	Timothy Fitzgerald	Head	67	Tinman	Ireland
	Mary Ann Fitzgerald	Daughter	15	-	Ireland
	James Halflan	Lodger	48	Shoemaker	Ireland
	Julia Halflan	Wife	24	-	Ireland
Pleasant Street					
24	James Fleming	Lodger	22	Tailor	Dungarvan, Co.Waterford

	Laurence Fleming	Lodger	21	Mason	Dungarvan, Co. Waterford
27	James McCormack	Head	55	Stone Mason	Dublin
	Mary McCormack	Wife	56	Maid of all work	Cork
	Bat Meehan	Lodger	30	Baker	Cork
	John Walsh	Lodger	26	Labourer	Mylough, Connaught
	Mary Walsh	Wife	28	Dressmaker	Donmore, Co. Waterford
	Jeramiah Collins	-	36	Labourer	Tipareary
	Ellen Collins	Wife	47	Dressmaker	Clanmore
	James Caltey	-	28	Labourer	Cork
	Michael Can	-	35	Labourer	Warren Pt., Co. Down
	Mary Can	Wife	34	Dressmaker	Warren Pt., Co. Down
	James White	-	45	Weaver	Rosstrevor, Co. Down
Welcome Street					
2	Bridget Manro	-	21	Soldiers wife	Tralee, Kerry
	Hannah Manro	Daughter	1	-	Portsmouth
	Elizabeth Finn	-	50	-	Carlow
	Thomas Feneighly	Head	23	Private 77th Regt	Dingle, Kerry
	Mary Feneighly	Wife	23	-	Dingle, Kerry
	Joanna Feneighly	Daughter	18 mths		Dowlais
	Joanna Julian	Lodger	25	Wife of Pvt. 77th Regt.	Listowell, Kerry
Worcester Place Barracks					
	Robert Savage	-	43	Barrack Sgt. Major/ Chelsea Pensioner	Ireland
	Elizabeth Savage	Wife	35	-	America
	Elizabeth Ann Savage	Daughter	17	-	Ireland
	Rachel Jane Savage	Daughter	10	Scholar	Portsmouth
	Emma Louise Savage	Daughter	9	Scholar	Lancashire
	Robert Henry Savage	Son	5	-	Kent
	Martha Amelia Savage	Daughter	2	-	Swansea
Postern					
	Michael Harison		20	Private 77th Regiment	Co. Kerry
	Daniel Charley		22	Private 77th Regiment	Co. Kerry

Philip Stokes	25	Private 77th Regiment	Tipperary
Bernard Gilchrist	23	Private 77th Regiment	Tyrone
Henry Lofttas	25	Private 77th Regiment	Tyrone
Thomas Gilchrist	32	Private 77th Regiment	Tyrone
Mathew Cromwell	21	Private 77th Regiment	Kerry
Denis Naughton	21	Private 77th Regiment	Mill Town, Kerry
Stewart Ritchie	33	Private 77th Regiment	Derry
Patrick Conlan	32	Private 77th Regiment	Dublin
John Murphy	23	Private 77th Regiment	Kerry
George Graham	28	Private 77th Regiment	Sligo
Thomas Hurleahy	21	Private 77th Regiment	Tipperary
Thomas Moore	32	Private 77th Regiment	Galway
William Spencer	21	Private 77th Regiment	Tipperary
Robert Jamison	22	Private 77th Regiment	Dublin
John Quinlan	24	Private 77th Regiment	Kerry
Patrick Tonlan	23	Private 77th Regiment	Tipperary
John Halflan	24	Private 77th Regiment	Tipperary
Wiliam Caldwell	25	Private 77th Regiment	Co. Antrim
Thomas McGrath	25	Private 77th Regiment	Co. Tipperary
Michael Daly	34	Private 77th Regiment	Westmeath
John Tobin	23	Private 77th Regiment	Bellingary
Anthony Killough	33	Private 77th Regiment	Galway
Patrick Connell	27	Private 77th Regiment	Galway
Michael Hogan	24	Private 77th Regiment	Kerry
Thomas Kennedy	23	Private 77th Regiment	Tipperary
James McGhee	38	Private 77th Regiment	Kilkenny
Edward Gonimane	22	Private 77th Regiment	Tipperary
James Morris	32	Private 77th Regiment	Tipperary
John Loftas	28	Private 77th Regiment	Limerick
Robert Southgate	38	Colour Sgt. 77th Regiment	Suffolk
Thomas Hock	37	Colour Sgt. 77th Regiment	Somerset
Wiliam Bowden	33	Colour Sgt. 77th Regiment	Norfolk
James Murphy	37	Private 77th Regiment	Cork
Robert Stace	29	Corporal 77th Regiment	Suffolk
James Marlston	28	Private 77th Regiment	Dublin
John Mooney	30	Private 77th Regiment	Mayo
James Jayce	24	Private 77th Regiment	Galway

High Street (off Davies Court) and (off Regent Court)

Bridget Miles	-	16	Servant	Waterford
Martin McHugh	Lodger	20	Labourer	Galway
John Hughes	Head	25	Labourer	Cork
Francis Burns	-	30	Labourer, Excavating	Ireland

Michael Burns	-	18	Labourer, Excavating	Ireland
James Kelly	-	27	Labourer, Excavating	Ireland
Michael Barke	-	-	Mariner	Ireland
Howell Court				
Megean Sullivan	Head	30	Hawker	Kilmore, Kerry
Mary Sullivan	Wife	25	-	Kilmore, Kerry
Dorothy Sullivan	Mother	50	-	Kilmore, Kerry
Margaret Sullivan	Daughter	22	Stocking Maker	Kilmore, Kerry
Elizabeth Donovan	Lodger	26	Female Servant	Rosscarbery, Cork
Mary O'Coner	Lodger	20	Soldiers Wife	Dingle
James O'Coner	Son	3	-	Co. Cork
William O'Coner	Son	3 mths	-	Dowlais
High Street				
John Kelly	Lodger	40	Hawker	Ireland
Margaret Kelly	Wife	28	-	Ireland
Thomas O'Bryan	-	30	Shoemaker	Ireland
Catherine O'Bryan	Wife	38	-	Ireland
John Prendergast	Head	30	Hawker	Co. Mayo
Margaret Prendergast	Wife	26	-	Bristol
Bridget Prendergast	Daughter	6	-	Cardiff
Ellen Prendergast	Daughter	3	-	Swansea
Thomas Prendergast	Son	1	-	Swansea
Ellen Drescol	-	14	Servant	Cork
Thomas Doharly	Lodger	38	-	Co. Kildare
Jeremiah Finns	Lodger	40	-	Limerick
Baptist Court				
John Duggan	Lodger	27	Bookseller	Ireland
Orchard Street				
20 Thos. Thornton	Visitor	19	Labourer	Ireland
24 Henry McGuin	Lodger	23	Seaman	Ireland
David Court				
John Courtney	Head	38	Cordwainer	Ireland
Susan Courtney	Wife	35	-	Ireland
Louisa Courtney	Daughter	8	-	Swansea
David Courtney	Son	1	-	Swansea
Owen Row				
Mary Linard	Head	46	Umbrella Maker	Tipperary

	Name	Relation	Age	Occupation	Birthplace
	Ellen Linard	Daughter	23	-	Swansea
	Mary Linard	Daughter	13	-	Swansea
	John Bonnell	Lodger	30	-	Cork
	Patrick Bonnell	Lodger	24	-	Merthyr
Queen Street					
26	Patrick Ahern	Head	32	Labourer	Co. Cork
	Cathrine Ahern	Wife	30	-	Co. Cork
	John Ahern	Son	5	Scholar	Co. Cork
	Johanna Ahern	Daughter	1	-	Co. Cork
28	Thomas Driscoll	Head	45	Plasterer	Ireland
	Margaret Driscoll	Wife	40	-	Ireland
	Ellinor Driscoll	Daughter	13	-	Ireland
	William Driscoll	Son	9	-	Ireland
Bowen Court					
3	Jemmima Thoms	-	-	Milkmaid	Ireland
Padley's Yard					
	Timothy Mahony	Head	40	Wheelwright	Ireland
	Jeremi Mahony	Son	15	Errand boy	Ireland
	+ 3 children	-	5 - 14	-	Ireland
	Johanna Ahern	-	50	Servant	Ireland
Strand					
20	John Scot	Head	39	Innkeeper of the "Packet Hotel"	Ireland
	Elizabeth Scot	Wife	37	-	Cornwall
	J. James Scot	Son	9	Scholar	Ireland
27	James Byrnes	Head	27	Victler	Ireland
	Susan Byrnes	Wife	26	-	Ireland
	Eliza Byrnes	Daughter	7 mths	-	Swansea
	Edward Byrnes	Relative	20	Labourer	Ireland
	Charles Smith	Visitor	21	Labourer	Ireland
	Wiliam Rock	-	20	Servant	Ireland
	Miles Oweny	-	-	Tailor	Cork
	John Heakey	Head	27	Labourer	Adare, Co. Limerick
	Mary Heakey	Wife	25	-	Ballyhoien, Co. Cork
	Michael Sweney	B-in-law	6	At home	Swansea
	Miles Sweney	Head	58	Tailor	Cork
	Cathrine Sweney	Wife	47	-	Cork
	Cathrine Sweney	Daughter	21	At home	Cork
	John Sweney	Son	14	-	Swansea
	Miles Sweney	Son	10	-	Swansea

Ellen Sweney	Daughter	12	-	Swansea
Edward Sweney	Son	9	-	Swansea
Ebenezer Street				
Patrick McAuley	Visitor	42	Pedler	Ireland
Johanna McAuley	Wife	41	-	Ireland
James Murray	Visitor	35	Bootmaker	Ireland
Tontine Street				
Margaret Brine	Head	60	Pauper	Ireland
Mathew Street				
Hugh McDonald	Head	49	Railway Labourer	Co. Down
Elizabeth McDonald	Wife	49	-	Co. Down
John McDonald	Son	24	-	Co. Down
Henry McDonald	Son	22	-	Co. Down
James Burns	-	24	Railway Labourer	Dublin
Patrick Kelly	-	24	Railway Labourer	Westmeath
Pottery Street				
Mary Fitzgerald	Lodger	30	-	Waterford
Joseph Fitzgerald	Son	9 mths	-	Swansea
William Fitzgerald	Son	9 mths	-	Swansea
Powell Street				
1 John Callagin	Head	32	-	Cork
Hannah Callagin	Wife	22	-	Cork
Samuel Hart	Head	69	Shoemaker	Ireland
Mary Hart	Wife	68	-	Swansea
John Hart	Son	28	Labourer	Ireland
Bridget Hart	G-daught.	2	-	Swansea
Jockey Street				
James Galagan	Head	42	Chelsea Pensioner	Ireland
Margaret Galagan	Wife	34	-	Ireland
Francis Galagan	Son	7	-	Newcastle T.
Jane Galagan	Daughter	6	-	Gosport
John Galagan	Son	4	-	Carmarthen
Elizabeth Galagan	Daughter	2	-	Llanelly
North Court				
Michael Leahy	Head	24	Labourer	Ireland
Ann Leahy	Wife	20	-	Swansea
John Leahy	Son	6 mths	-	Swansea
St John Street				
John Appleyard	Head	28	Labourer	Ireland
Mary Appleyard	Wife	26	-	Ireland
John Appleyard	Son	4	-	Bristol
Patrick Appleyard	Son	3	-	Bristol

	Name	Relation	Age	Occupation	Birthplace
	Ann Lynch	M-in-Law	66	-	Ireland
	John Cox	Lodger	34	Labourer	Ireland
	Catherine Cox	Wife	47	-	Ireland
	Michael Riordan	Head	34	Shoemaker	Cork
	Catharine Riordan	Wife	33	-	Cork
	Bridget Riordan	Daughter	10	-	Cork
	Patrick Riordan	Son	9	-	Cork
	Michael Riordan	Son	2	-	Cork
	Mary Riordan	Daughter	3	-	Bridgend
	Catharine Riordan	Daughter	1 mth	-	Swansea
	William Welsh	Lodger	20	Labourer	Ireland
Eliphant Street					
	Peter Hagady	Head	46	Labourer	Ireland
	Mary Hagady	Wife	60	-	Pembroke
	James Nuwgent	Lodger	23	Porter	Dublin
	Hannah Nuwgent	Lodger	26	-	Pembroke
	James Nuwgent	Son	18 mths	-	Pembroke
Greenhill Street					
	Michael Shanahan	Head	30	Common Labourer	Mitchaltown, Co. Cork
	Ellen Shanahan	Daughter	6	At home	Mitchaltown, Co. Cork
	Daniel Shanahan	Son	4	-	Swansea
	Margaret Shanahan	Daughter	2	-	Swansea
	Ellen Weles	M-in-Law	50	House Keeper	Michaltown, Co. Cork
	Daniel Shanahan	Father	64	Alms	Co. Cork
	Margaret Shanahan	Mother	72	Alms	Co. Cork
	Thomas Shanahan	Brother	38	Common Labourer	Co. Cork
12	Patrick Brian	Head	50	Common Labourer	Cork
	Abby Brian	Wife	40	-	Cork
	Mary Brian	Daughter	14	-	Swansea
	Joanna Brian	Daughter	6 mths	-	Swansea
	Samuel Ford	Head	45	Shoemaker	Kilmadry, Cork
	Margaret Ford	Wife	40	-	Klinty
	William Ford	Son	20	Shoemaker	Kilty
	Robert Ford	Son	15	-	Monmouthshire
	Stephen Ford	Son	12	-	Swansea
	Henry Ford	Son	8	-	Swansea
	Samuel Ford	Son	6	-	Tredegar
	Daniel O'Brien	Head	26	Copperworks Labourer	Clonakilty

Mary O'Brien	Wife	27	-	Clonakilty
Patrick McCarthy	Lodger	32	Common Labourer	Clonakilty
Mary McCarthy	Lodger	35	-	Tipperary
Julia O'Brien	Lodger	50	Charwoman	Clanakily
John London	Lodger	35	Common Labourer	Tipperary
Denis Murphy	Head	30	Dock Labourer	Mill Street, Co. Cork
Eliza Murphy	Wife	32	-	Swansea
John Murphy	Son	11 mths	-	Swansea
John Hanley	Lodger	22	Common Labourer	Bantry, Co. Cork
John Karrig	Lodger	26	Common Labourer	Tulla, Co. Clare
Barnard McCann	Lodger	24	Common Labourer	Ballynahinch, Co. Down
Edmund Barry	Lodger	26	Common Labourer	Fermoy Co. Cork
John Porter	Head	46	Pedlar, Dealer in Rags and Bones	Hillsborough, Co. Down
Isabella Porter	Wife	31	-	Co. Down
Robert Porter	Son	21	-	Brecon
Patrick Kenevan	Head	64	Shoemaker	Limerick
Margaret Kenivan	Wife	25	-	Mitchelstown, Cork
William Kenivan	Son	4	-	Mitchelstown, Cork
Catherine Kenivan	Daughter	1	-	Swansea
Maurice Scanlon	Head	45	Cartman	Listowel, Kerry
Nance Scanlon	Wife	39	-	Bettws, Glam
Daniel Scanlon	Son	17	Common Labourer	Swansea
+ 5 children	-	-	-	Swansea
Maurice Scanlon	Lodger	47	Common Labourer	Lugullin
Daniel Scanlon	Lodger	20	Common Labourer	Listowel, Kerry
Johanna Stack	Servant	27	House Servant	Listowl, Kerry
Charles Gwirk	Lodger	60	Labourer in Hafod Copperworks	Kildalkey
Patrick Henivan	Head	44	Shoemaker	Limerick, Bragy
Margaret Henivan	Wife	25	-	Mitchelstown, Cork

Willian Henivan	Son	4	-	Mitchelstown, Cork
Catharine Henivan	Daughter	1	-	Swansea
Dinis Lane	Head	67	Blacksmith, disabled	Liskill, Cork
Ellen Lane	Wife	56	-	Kanturk, Cork
Anne Lane	Daughter	14	At home	Risca, Mons.
Roger Collins	Head	43	Whitesmith	Clasmore
Mary Collins	Wife	42	-	Clasmore
Bridget Collins	Daughter	17	At home	Newport, Mons.
Ellin Collins	Daughter	15	At home	Swansea
+ 5 children		4 -13	-	Pembroke/ Brecon
Jeremiah Dempsy	Head	45	Common Labourer	Roscarbery, Cork
Mary Ann Dempsy	-	16	At home	Buckinghamshire
Charlotte Dempsy	-	14	-	Buckinghamshire
Ellen Dempsy	-	12	-	Swansea
+ 3 other children	-	-	-	Swansea
Timothy Fling	-	35	Railway Labourer	Glanmire, Cork
Mary Fling	-	40	-	Ballybrick, Cork
Michael Fling	-	11	Scholar	Rathewenny, Cork
James Higgins	Head	40	Common Labourer	Ireland
Catharine Higgins	Wife	31	-	Ireland
Arthur Leary	Head	54	Dock Labourer	Clashmore, Waterford
Bridget Leary	Wife	42	-	Clashmore, Waterford
Edward Leary	Son	17	-	Clashmore, Waterford
Arthur Leary	Son	5	-	-
John Leary	Son	-	-	-
Maurice Carthy	Lodger	26	Labourer	Youghal, Cork
Ellen Carthy	Wife	24	-	Youghal, Cork
Denis Lucy	Lodger	31	Labourer	Drishawe
Charles Crowley	Head	28	Wire Worker	Bristol
Ann Crowley	Wife	28	Lodging Housekeeper	Bristol

Charles Crowley	Son	11	-	Bristol
Edward McEvery	Lodger	36	Hatter	Dublin
Susan McEvery	Wife	26	-	Cardiff
Emily McEvery	Daughter	-	-	Halifax
Edward Donovan	Visitor	30	Hatter	Bath
Anne Donovan	Wife	35	-	Llanidloes
Cross Court				
Ellen Leary	Head	55	Pauper	Cork
Mary Leary	Daughter	16	Pedler	Cork
Ellen Leary	Daughter	14	At home	Cork
Ann Leary	Daughter	12	At home	Swansea
+ 4 other children	-	3 - 10	At home	Swansea
William Gogen	Lodger	23	Common Labourer	Cork
Bridge Street				
Timothy Leany	Head	51	Copperman	Cork
Mary Leany	Wife	45	-	Cork
Cornelius Leany	Son	19	Copperman	Sussex
John Leany	Son	17	Labourer	Cork
+ 3 children	-	11-15	-	Cork
+ 3 children	-	2-9	-	Swansea
Edmund Keating	Head	36	Copperman	Bog of Allen
Ann Keating	Wife	35	Dressmaker	Cappaquin, Cork
Elizabeth Keating	Daughter	12	Scholar	Swansea
James Keating	Son	2	-	Swansea
Mary Quinlan	Visitor	30	Dressmaker	Cappaquin, Cork
Mary McDormant	Head	50	Alms	Rosscomon
Bridget Noonan	Visitor	20	House Labourer	Co. Limerick
Mary Ryan	-	84	Pauper	Ireland
Patrick Ivory	Head	39	Shoemaker	Tipperary
Elizabeth Ivory	Wife	40	-	Cork
Patrick Ivory	Son	10	At home	Devon
Edward Ivory	Son	4	-	Swansea
John Ivory	Son	-	-	Swansea
Daniel Logan	Visitor	40	Common Labourer	Dumfries
Jery Crowly	Lodger	18	Common Labourer	Waterford
Patrick Sherry	Lodger	40	Common Labourer	Dublin
June Mitchell	Wife	30	-	Dublin
Peter Sherry	Son	12	-	Dublin
John Sherry	Son	10	-	Scotland
Daniel Sherry	Son	7	-	Dumfries

Denis Ryan	-	30	Common Labourer	Tipperary
Julia Kenacy	Wife	26	-	Tipperary
Raphael Ryan	Son	1	-	Monmouthshire
Richard Fitzgibbon	Lodger	27	Traveller & Locksmith	Co. Limerick
Hanora Fitzgibbon	Daughter	17	-	Co. Limerick
Well Street				
Patrick McTigue	Head	36	Commn Labourer	Galway
Bridget McTigue	Wife	34	-	Galway
3 children	-	4-9	Home	Galway
Bridgitt McTigue	Daughter	1	-	Swansea
Timothy Sullivan	Lodger	46	Labourer	Cork
John Sullivan	Son	13	-	Cork
Michael Sullivan	Son	6	-	Cork
Daniel MacCarty	Head	62	Matchseller (blind)	Roscarbery
Catherine MacCarty	Wife	50	-	Roscarbery
Gery MacCarty	Son	24	Common Labourer	Roscarbery
Michael MacCarty	Son	18	Common Labourer	Roscarbery
Mary MacCarty	Daughter	2	-	Swansea
John Wades	Visitor	40	Common Labourer	Co. Clare
Margaret Wades	Wife	32	-	Co. Clare
Anora Casy	Head	50	Alms, sickly	Tipperary
Daniel Buckly	head	40	Common Labourer	Kinsale, Cork
Abby Buckly	Wife	32	-	Kinsale, Cork
Catharine Buckly	Daughter	13	home	Swansea
+ 4 other children	-	3-10	Home	Swansea
Elizabeth Holran	Head	44	Pauper	Dunrale
Kate Holran	Daughter	15	Charwoman	Cork
Timothy Holran	Son	11	Mason boy	Swansea
+ 2 other children	-	5 & 7	Home	Swansea
James Canty	Head	50	Common Labourer	Ireland
Margaret Canty	Wife	50	-	Ireland
William Burns	Lodger	29	Common Labourer	Ireland
James Burns	Son	7	-	Swansea
Green Row				
Thomas Henwright	Head	45	Copperwork Labourer	Gale, Co. Kerry
Mary Henwright	Wife	35	Housekeeper	Bath
Ellen Henwright	Daughter	10	Home	Swansea
Patrick Sheen	Lodger	35	Pensioner	Co. Kerry
Catharine Sheen	Wife	30	-	Co. Kerry
Kate Sheen	Daughter	-	-	Swansea
Catharine Leary	Daughter	28	-	Dunmanway, Cork

Bat Leary	S-in-Law	35	Common Labourer	Dunmanway, Cork
Kate Mahony	-	60	Alms	Dunmanway, Cork
Michael Leary	-	4	Deaf and dumb	Dunmanway, Cork
Peggy Copiley	-	30	Fishwoman	Dunmanway, Cork
Edmund Barry	Head	35	Carpenter	Ballyhooley, Cork
Elizabeth Barry	Wife	32	-	Ballyhooley, Cork
John Barry	Son	16	-	Ballyhooley, Cork
Elizabeth Barry	-	12	-	Ballyhooley, Cork
David Barry	-	9	Home	Ballyhooley, Cork
Michael Callighan	Lodger	33	Common Labourer	Ballyhooley, Cork
Hounora Callighan	Wife	33	-	Ballyhooley, Cork
+ 3 children	-	5-10	-	Ireland
Dinis Murphy	-	27	Common Labourer	Castletown Roch
Ellen Murphy	Wife	28	-	Castletown, Roch
Jeremiah O'Brien	Head	36	Railway Labourer	Clanakilty, Cork
Mary O'Brien	Wife	40	-	Clanakilty, Cork
+ 4 children	-	3-12	Home	Clanakilty, Cork
Richard Tobin	Lodger	26	Railway Labourer	Bandon, Cork
Peggy Tobin	Wife	30	-	Bandon, Cork
James Tobin	Son	10	Home	Bandon, cork
Mary Tobin	Daughter	4	Home	Bandon, Cork
Michael Tobin	Son	1	-	Swansea
Michae Calhan	Lodger	30	Beggar	Cashel Ventry, Cork
Michael Calhan	Lodger	23	Servant	Cashel Ventry, Cork
John Macarty	Lodger	20	Common Labourer	Co. Kerry
Judy Macarty	Wife	40	Workwoman	Co. Kerry
Darby Shea	-	40	Buyer of rags & bones	Co. Kerry
Michael Shea	Son	16	-	Co. Kerry
Thomas Aherne	Head	46	Copperman	Tipperary
Mary Aherne	Wife	38	-	Cornwall
Timothy Aherne	Son	15	Copper Labourer	Swansea
+ 2 children	-	2 & 13	Scholars	Swansea
Mill Street				
Laurance Meany	Head	49	Copperman	Ireland
Mary Meany	Wife	50	-	Ireland
Bridgit Meany	Daughter	14	Home	Reigate, Surrey
Ellen Meany	Daughter	11	Home	Swansea
John Meany	Son	8	-	Swansea

Hannah O'Brien	-	18	House Servant	Ireland
James Walsh	Head	34	Copperman	Kildany, Cork
Mary Walsh	Wife	31	-	Kildany, Cork
Thomas Walsh	Son	10	Home	Swansea
+ 2 other children	-	3-5	Home	Swansea
Michael Curtin	Lodger	30	Labourer	Blackpool, Cork
Daniel Shea	Lodger	24	Labourer	Mallow
James Doherty	Lodger	16	Labourer	Mitchelstown
Thomas Flyn	Head	23	Labourer	Mitchelstown, Cork
Mary Flyn	Wife	22	-	Glanaorth, Cork
Ellen Flyn	Daughter	7 mths	-	Swansea
Catherine Barry	Visitor	25	House Servant	Glannorth, Cork
Hanorah Lahy	Lodger	25	-	Glanvill
Patrick Doherty	Lodger	26	Labourer	Mitchelstown
Mary Doherty	Wife	24	-	Mitchelstown
Thomas Doherty	Son	3	-	Swansea
Jeremiah O'Neil	Head	48	Hawker	Ireland
Elinor O'Neil	Daughter	24	-	Swansea
William Stack	Lodger	30	Labourer	Ireland
Mary Stack	Wife	22	-	Swansea
Patrick O'Neil	Son	17	Labourer	Swansea
Daniel Sulivan	Head	43	Labourer	Killaghanagh, Cork
Margaret Sulivan	Wife	34	-	Killaghanagh, Cork
Mary Sulivan	Daughter	12	-	Killaghanagh, Cork
Johanah Sulivan	Daughter	10	-	Swansea
John Sulivan	Son	8	-	Swansea
+ 2 other children	-	-	-	Swansea
Johana Sulivan	Mother	68	-	Killaghanagh, Cork
Flint Row				
John Corkran	Head	40	Copperworks Labourer	Brenny, Cork
Hanoreh Corkran	Wife	46	-	Brenny, Cork
Ellen Corkran	Daughter	20	Home	Brenny, Cork
Jane Corkran	Daughter	14	Copperwoman	Kent
Saml. Gogan	Lodger	60	River Labourer	Skibereen, Cork
John Gogan	Lodger	34	Quarryman	Skibereen, Cork
Mary Gogan	Wife	31	-	Skibereen, Cork
Greenhill High Street				
John White	Head	40	Copperman	Ireland
Mary White	Wife	35	-	Ireland
Jeremiah White	Son	16	Ladler	Ireland
Ellen White	Daughter	10	Scholar	Ireland

+ 2 children	-	6 & 8	Scholars	Ireland
Harriet White	Daughter	2	Home	Swansea
Daniel O'Brien	Visitor	50	Sailor	Ireland
Charles Foley	Lodger	45	Labourer	Ireland
Laurence McLaughlin	Lodger	48	Labourer	Ireland
Richard Daly	Lodger	40	Labourer	Ireland
Marty Fitzgerald	Lodger	42	Labourer	Ireland
John Keilly	Visitor	27	Labourer	Ireland
Lewis Court				
Jeremiah Shean	Head	28	Labourer	Kerry
Mary Shean	Wife	30	-	Kerry
Catharine Shean	Daughter	2	-	Swansea
Patrick Shean	Brother	27	Labourer	Kerry
Catharine Shean	S-in-law	29	-	Kerry
David Marra	Visitor	19	Labourer	Cork
Thomas Murphy	Head	25	Railway Labourer	Cork
Jane Murphy	Wife	22	-	Swansea
Greyhound Street				
Denis Collins	Head	26	Gardener	Bandon, Cork
Margaret Collins	Wife	17	-	Kinneth, Cork
Lamb Croft				
Ellen Sullivan	Head	50	Dealer/Pedling	Cork
Timothy Sullivan	Son	19	Painter	Cork
Hanora Ryan	Relation	60	-	Tipperary
Thomas Murray	Lodger	22	Labourer	Arrnore, Waterford
Alice Murray	Wife	29	-	Lismore, Waterford
Denis Bournes	Head	45	Labourer	Cork
Johanna Bournes	Wife	32	-	Cork
Ellen Bournes	-	11	_	Swansea
+ 4 other children	-	1-9	-	Swansea
Timothy Myrin	F-in-law	64	Coal Hewer	Cork
John Shea	Head	36	Copperworks Labourer	Cork
Margaret Shea	Wife	35	-	Cork
Jeremiah Cobin	Visitor	26	Common Labourer	Cork
Michael Ryan	Visitor	30	Common Labourer	Tipperary
John Welsh	-	26	Common Labourer	Cork
James Costley	-	36	Common Labourer	Kilkenny
Timothy Connell	-	22	Common Labourer	Cork
Cornelius Leary	-	21	Common Labourer	Kerry

Daniel Sullivan	-	19	Common Labourer	Kerry
Mary Leary	-	12	House Servant	Kerry
Croft (near Baptist Meeting House)				
Edward Casey	Head	41	Labourer	Ireland
Margaret Casey	Wife	36	Housekeeper	Glamorgan
Elese Casey	Daughter	10	-	Glamorgan
Ellen Casey	Daughter	1	-	Glamorgan
Thomas Owens	Visitor	19	Labourer	Glamorgan
Hugh Doyle	Visitor	21	Labourer	Ireland
Denis Skully	Visitor	22	Labourer	Ireland
John Brien	Visitor	28	Labourer	Ireland
John Heffren	Visitor	30	Labourer	Ireland
Upper Davatty Street				
John Brien	Head	30	Common Labourer	Cork
Margaret Brien	Wife	28	-	Cork
John Brien	Son	2	-	Glamorgan
Catharine Foley	Lodger	48	Pedler	Cork
Julia Foley	Lodger	14	House Servant	Cork
Davatty Street				
Catherine Mulky	Head	30	Green Grocer	Dungarvan, Waterford
James Quarry	Visitor	26	Shoemaker	Dungarvan, Waterford
Bridget Fitzgerald	-	26	House Servant	Dungarvan, Waterford
High Street				
William Garde	Head	33	Officer of Customs	Ireland
Mary Garde	Wife	26	-	Swansea
Mary Dower	Niece	2	Scholar	Swansea
Elizabeth Jane Bullin	Niece	10	Scholar	Swansea
Elizabeth Jeffereys	-	24	House Servant	Carmarthen
Thomas Fox	Head	41	Master Shoemaker	Cork
Charlotte Fox	Wife	42	-	Swansea
Thomas Fox	Son	18	-	Swansea
Mary Fox	Daughter	17	-	Cork
+ 5 other children	-	2-12	-	Swansea
New Street				
39 William Cassidy	Head	30	Cabinet Maker	Ireland
Catharine Cassidy	Wife	27	-	Ireland
Isabelle Cassidy	Daughter	8	Scholar	Ireland
George Cassidy	Son	3	-	Ireland
Alexander Cassidy	Son	1	-	Swansea

48	William Todd	Head	40	Servant	Hillsborough, Co. Down
	Mary Todd	Wife	36	Laundress	Clifford, Hereford
	Mary Ann Todd	Daughter	12	Scholar	Canada
Tudor Court					
	Thomas Newport	head	35	Blacksmith	Bristol
	Bridget Newport	Wife	30	-	Cove of Cork
	+ 2 daughters	-	8-10	-	Bristol
	Bridget Newport	Daughter	8	-	Swansea
	John Newport	Son	2	-	Swansea
	Margaret Newport	Mother	60	-	Wexford
Dyvatty Street					
	Thomas Bride	Head	63	Labourer	Cork
	Elen Bride	Wife	56	Domestic Servant	Cork
	John Bride	Son	27	Labourer	Cork
	+ 2 other sons	-	20 & 24	Labourers	Cork
	+ 2 Daughters	-	15 & 18	Dressmakers	Cork
High Street					
	Michael Spilman	Head	36	Cord Wainder	Co. Galway
	Ann Spilman	Wife	40	-	Pembroke
	Nicholas Parkes	Lodger	28	Railway Labourer	Waterford
	Jeremiah Gahaern	Lodger	20	Cord Wainder	Cork
	James Brien	Lodger	28	Cord Wainder	Dublin
	John Kennedy	Lodger	22	Cord Wainder	Kildare
	Thomas Burke	Lodger	28	Cord Wainder	Tipperary
Willow Street					
	Terry McCarthy	Head	24	Weaver	Cork
	Catharine McCarthy	Wife	29	-	Cork
Charles Street					
	William Bayly	Lodger	22	Labourer	Ireland
	Patrick Branan	Lodger	26	Labourer	Ireland
	Catharine Branan	Lodger	26	-	Ireland
	Mary Ann Branan	Lodger	31	-	Wigan
	John Murphy	Head	41	Labourer	Ireland
	Hanora Murphy	Wife	35	-	Ireland
	William Murphy	Son	11	-	Swansea
	+ 2 sons	-	2 & 8	-	Swansea
	Catharine Gorman	Lodger	22	Hawker	Ireland
	James Murry	Head	30	Wire Worker	Ireland
	Ann Murry	Wife	48	-	Ireland
	James Murry	Son	15	Labourer	Ireland
	Mary Murry	Daughter	16	-	Swansea

Catharine Murry	Daughter	14	-	Swansea
John Coly	Lodger	33	Sailor	Ireland
Ann Coly	Wife	28	-	Ireland
Catharine Coly	Daughter	9	At home	Swansea
James Cafrey	Lodger	29	Labourer	Ireland
Catharine Cafrey	Wife	30	-	Ireland
+ 2children	-	6 & 8	-	Ireland
James Cafrey	Son	2	-	Swansea
James Donel	Lodger	31	Tinman	Ireland
Willliam Roach	Lodger	40	Tinman	Ireland
Michael Regan	Lodger	28	Tinman	Ireland
Honora Regan	Wife	26	-	Ireland
Timothy Coughlin	Head	58	Labourer	Cork
Johanna Coughlin	Wife	57	-	Cork
Mary Coughlin	Daughter	20	-	Kilmore
Daniel Collins	Lodger	40	Labourer	Ireland
Denis Mahony	Lodger	28	Labourer	Ireland
Catharine Leary	Head	37	Widow	Ireland
Cornelius Leary	Son	9	-	Swansea
Denis Leary	Son	5	-	Swansea
William Ponsonby	Head	36	Copperman	Ireland
Margaret Ponsonby	Wife	30	-	Ireland
Catharine Ponsonby	Daughter	10	-	Swansea
Mary Ponsonby	Daughter	5	-	Swansea
Bridget Ponsonby	Mother	64	-	Ireland
Timothy Sullivan	Lodger	25	Labourer	Ireland
Hannah Keef	Lodger	28	House Servant	Ireland
James Sullivan	Head	35	Labourer	Ireland
Hanora Sullivan	Wife	32	-	Ireland
James Sullivan	Son	19	-	Swansea
+ 2 children	-	4 & 8	-	Swansea
Ellen Bryans	Lodger	60	-	Ireland
Catharine Sullivan	Lodger	46	Hawker	Ireland
Michael Sullivan	Lodger	23	Labourer	Ireland
Henry Shea	Lodger	50	Labourer	Ireland
Mary Shea	Wife	44	-	Ireland
James Sullivan	Lodger	26	Labourer	Ireland
James Deconry	Head	50	Labourer	Ireland
Ellin Deconry	Wife	45	-	Ireland
James Deconry	Son	19	Collier	Ireland
Daniel Deacey	Lodger	50	Labourer	Ireland
Johanna Deacey	Wife	56	-	Ireland

John Deacey	Son	20	Labourer	Ireland
+ 2 children	-	-	-	Ireland
Johanna Hade	Lodger	22	Labouring	Ireland
Jeremiah Mahony	Head	30	Labourer	Ireland
Mary Mahony	Wife	28	-	Ireland
Mary Mahony	Daughter	5	-	Ireland
John Dunavon	Lodger	52	Labourer	Ireland
Mary Dunavon	Wife	27	Hawker	Ireland
James Murray	Head	50	Tinman	Ireland
Ann Murray	Wife	48	-	Ireland
James Murray	Son	18	-	Wrexham
Mary Ann Murray	Daughter	16	-	Swansea
Catharine Murray	Daughter	14	-	Swansea
Thomas Coady	Lodger	33	Nailer	Ireland
Catharine Coady	Wife	28	-	Ireland
Ann Coady	Daughter	9	-	Swansea
James Casey	Head	29	Labourer	Ireland
Catharine Casey	Wife	30	-	Ireland
+ 2 children	-	6 & 8	-	Ireland
James Casey	Son	2	-	Swansea
James Donnel	Lodger	31	Tinman	Ireland
William Oak	Lodger	40	Labourer	Ireland
Richard Bowlan	Head	63	Glazer	Dublin
Mary Bowlan	Wife	57	-	Ireland
Richard Bowlan	Son	20	Labourer	Ireland
Susan Bowlan	Daughter	14	Scholar	Ireland
Bridget Bowlan	-	-	Washerwoman	Ireland
Hanora Cockrane	Head	60	Takes in Lodgers	Ireland
Patrick Cockrane	Son	22	Labourer	Ireland
+ 4 other children	-	11-18	-	Ireland
Morgan Cockrane	Son	4	-	Swansea
William Green	Lodger	25	Labourer	Ireland
Mary Green	Lodger	28	Servant	Ireland
Catherine Green	Lodger	19	Servant	Ireland
John Murphy	Head	34	Labourer	Cork
Margaret Murphy	Wife	31	-	Cork
Daniel Kelly	Head	30	Labourer	Ireland
Margaret Kelly	Wife	30	-	Ireland
Johanna Kelly	Lodger	50	-	Ireland
Thos. Brauder	Lodger	26	Labourer	Ireland
Mary Brauder	Wife	21	-	Ireland
Elizabeth Carty	Lodger	51	Hawking	Ireland

Denis Kelly	Son	8	-	Swansea
Morgan Brauder	-	12	-	Swansea
Richard Warner	Lodger	20	Labourer	Ireland
James Crowly	Head	45	Labourer	Ireland
Hanora Crowly	Wife	40	-	Ireland
Cornelius Crowly	Son	15	Labourer	Ireland
James Crowly	Son	13	Labourer	Ireland
James Murphy	Lodger	30	Labourer	Ireland
Hanora Crowly	Lodger	20	-	Ireland
Michael O'Neal	Lodger	34	Labourer	Ireland
Margaret O'Neal	Wife	34	-	Ireland
+ 2 children	-	6 & 8	-	Ireland
William O'Neal	Son	18 mths	-	Swansea
Cornelius Harlinton	Lodger	34	-	Cork
Mary Harlinton	Wife	36	-	Cork
John Hurly	-	10	-	Cork
Michael Hurly	-	6	-	Cork
John Nash	Head	39	Labourer	Cork
Hanora Nash	Wife	30	-	Cork
John Nash	Son	6	-	Cork
Anora Nash	Daughter	4	-	Swansea
James Linch	Head	50	Labourer	Cork
Denis Linch	Son	22	Labourer	Cork
+ 2 sons	-	19 & 20	Labourers	Cork
James Linch	Lodger	21	Labourer	Cork
Eleanor Linch	Lodger	45	-	Cork
+ 3 children	-	10-19	-	Cork
Timothy Sullivan	Lodger	-	Labourer	Cork
John Sullivan	Son	18	Labourer	Cork
Margaret Sullivan	Daughter	16	-	Cork
Catherine Cockrine	Lodger	19	-	Cork
Lucy McCarty	Lodger	40	-	Cork
Hannora McCarty	-	-	-	-
Cornelius Hurly	Head	40	Labourer	Cork
Catherine Hurly	Wife	30	-	Cork
Bridget Hurly	Daughter	14	-	Cork
Fredrick Hurly	Son	9	-	Cork
Catherine Hurly	Daughter	4	-	Cork
Timothy Linn	Lodger	38	-	Cork
Michael Kelly	Head	40	Labourer	Ireland
Elizabeth Kelly	Wife	29	-	Ireland
+ 3 children		-5 mths-12 yrs-		Ireland

Mary Fleming	Lodger	23	Servant	Carmarthen
Murphy Cheer	Head	50	Labourer	Ireland
Mary Cheer	Wife	44	-	Ireland
Timothy Sullivan	Head	60	Labourer	Ireland
Margaret Sullivan	Wife	54	-	Ireland
Margaret Sullivan	Daughter	21	Servant	Ireland
Johanna Sullivan	Daughter	19	Servant	Ireland
Daniel Deacey	Head	50	Labourer	Ireland
Johanna Deacey	Wife	50	-	Ireland
John Deacey	Son	20	Labourer	Ireland
Daniel Deacey	Son	14	Labourer	Ireland
Denis Mahony	Head	34	Labouring	Cork
Margaret Mahony	Wife	35	Labouring	Cork
+ 3 children	-	2-11	-	Cork
Timothy Dealy	Lodger	10	-	Ireland
John Neel	Lodger	30	Labourer	Ireland
John Butterworth	Head	69	Labourer	Ireland
Catherine Butterworth	Wife	67	-	Ireland
Catherine Butterworth	Daughter	14	-	Ireland
Denis Heare	Lodger	24	Labouring	Ireland
John Wavin	Lodger	30	Labouring	Ireland
Christopher Allen	Head	38	Labouring	Ireland
Johanna Allen	Wife	30	-	Ireland
James Allen	Son	1	-	Maynouth
Thos. Sextine	Head	32	Labourer	Ireland
Margaret Sextine	Wife	35	-	Ireland
Thomas Sextine	Son	3	-	Swansea
Michael Regan	Head	28	Labourer	Ireland
Hannora Regan	Wife	26	-	Ireland
Johanna Brayan	Widow	-	-	Ireland
Catherine Brayan	-	16	Servant	Ireland
Daniel Driscol	Lodger	25	Labourer	Ireland
Nancy Driscol	Wife	21	-	Ireland
Mary Driscol	Daughter	1	-	Swansea
Timothy Cain	Head	40	Labourer	Ireland
Eleanor Cain	Wife	40	-	Ireland
+ 4 children	-	5 - 13	-	Ireland
Patrick Hannagh	Head	29	Labourer	Ireland
Eleanor Hannagh	-	26	-	Ireland
+ 2 sons	-	2 & 5	-	Ireland
Eleanor Hannagh	Daughter	1	-	Swansea
Denis Rock	Head	25	Labourer	Ireland

Judith Rock	Wife	29	-	Ireland
Eleanor Rock	Daughter	5	-	Ireland
Michael Killany	Head	28	Labourer	Ireland
Mary Killany	Wife	23	-	Ireland
Briget Killany	Daughter	1	-	Swansea
Michael Kelfry	Head	30	Labourer	Ireland
Eleanor Kelfry	Wife	30	-	Ireland
John Kelfrey	Son	7	-	Ireland
Ann Kelfrey	Daughter	6	-	Swansea
Michael Kelfrey	Son	2 mths	-	Swansea
Thomas Dealey	Head	37	Labourer	Swansea
Margaret Dealey	Wife	35	-	Ireland
+ 4 children	-	1 - 14	-	Ireland
Thomas Garran	Lodger	34	Labourer	Ireland
John Trawich	Lodger	34	Labourer	Ireland
Michael Cockran	Head	24	Labourer	Cork
Ellen Cockran	Wife	20	-	Cork
Timothy Hughgree	Lodger	22	Labourer	Ireland
Morgan Corkan	Lodger	19	-	Cork
Wm. Gannegill	Lodger	23	-	Cork
Ellin Cockrane	Lodger	19	-	Cork
Patrick Bute	Lodger	45	-	Cork
Margaret Bute	Lodger	25	-	Cork
Patrick Corkrane	-	19	-	Cork
Margaret Corkrane	-	16	-	Cork
Mary Brant	-	84	-	Cork
Cornelius Brant	-	15	-	Cork
Mary Glason	Head	50	Keeper of Lodging House	Ireland
James Glason	Son	21	Labourer	Ireland
+ 3 other sons	-	4 - 15	Labourers	Ireland
Alice Bach	Lodger	20	Servant	Ireland
Denis O'Brien	Lodger	30	Labourer	Ireland
Patrick O'Brien	Lodger	28	Labourer	Ireland
Michael O'Brien	Lodger	21	Labourer	Ireland
Caroline Neale	Lodger	30	Hawker	Ireland
July Neale	Lodger	26	Servant	Ireland
Richard Meara	Lodger	30	Labourer	Ireland
John McCarty	Head	27	Labourer	Ireland
Eleanor McCarty	Wife	26	-	Ireland
James McCarty	Son	9	-	Swansea
John McCarty	Son	1	-	Swansea

Johanna Cafrey	Lodger	14	-	Ireland
Thomas Casey	Head	48	Labourer	Ireland
Cathrine Casey	Wife	45	-	Ireland
+ 2 children	-	17 & 19	-	Ireland
Margaret Casey	Daughter	14	Servant	Swansea
+ 3 children	-	3- 12	-	Swansea
William Daniel	Head	35	Labourer	Ireland
Daniel Daniel	Son	8	-	Ireland
Catherine Daniel	Daughter	5	-	Swansea
Bat Driscol	Lodger	48	Labourer	Ireland
Elen Driscol	Wife	45	-	Ireland
James Driscol	Son	19	Labourer	Ireland
Jemima Meade	Lodger	22	Servant	Ireland
Mary Deecy	Lodger	22	Servant	Ireland
Silvester Harrington	Head	30	Labourer	Ireland
Ann Harrington	Wife	28	-	Ireland
Denis Harrington	Lodger	50	Whitesmith	Ireland
Cornelius Sillaven	Lodger	24	Labourer	Ireland
Mary Sillaven	-	2	-	Swansea
Margaret Halgin	Lodger	18	Servant	Ireland
Ann Halgin	Lodger	17	Servant	Ireland
Daniel O'Brayan	Lodger	27	Shoemaker	Ireland
Timothy Murphy	Lodger	21	-	Ireland
Denis Leary	Head	50	Labourer	Ireland
Ellin Leary	Wife	46	-	Ireland
Denis Leary	Son	21	-	Ireland
+ 5 children	-	8 - 19	-	Ireland
Julia Doyle	Lodger	25	Servant	Ireland
James Sillivan	Head	35	Labourer	Ireland
Hannora Sillivan	Wife	32	-	Ireland
+ 3 children	-	3 - 19	-	Ireland
Patrick Sillivan	Son	3 mths	-	Swansea
Elen Biagan	Lodger	50	Charring	Ireland
Catharine Filami	Lodger	46	Charring	Ireland
Michael Filami	Lodger	23	Labourer	Ireland
John Sillavan	Lodger	26	Labourer	Ireland
Michael Rogers	Lodger	25	Labourer	Ireland
Hannora Rogers	Wife	26	-	Ireland
Thomas Cody	Head	35	Nailer	Ireland
Ann Cody	Wife	28	-	Ireland
Catherine Cody	Daughter	9	-	Ireland

Emma Street

Henry Wardnes	Head	34	Labourer	Cork
Elizabeth Wardnes	Wife	26	-	Cork
+ 3 children	-	1 - 11	-	Cork
Bridget Fitzgerald	Lodger	22	Washerwoman	Cork
Margaret Butt	Lodger	40	Washerwoman	Cork
+ 2 sons	-	6 & 11	-	Cork
Ellen Dunavon	Lodger	28	Washerwoman	Cork
Michael Goney	Head	36	Labourer	Ireland
Catherine Goney	Wife	40	-	Ireland
Timothy Goney	Son	15	Labourer	Ireland
Nicholas Goney	Son	10	-	Swansea
John Whelan	Lodger	32	Labourer	Ireland
Mary Whelan	Wife	32	-	Ireland
+ 3 children	_	2 - 7	-	Ireland
Michael Mahony	Head	38	Labourer	Ireland
Mary Mahony	Wife	30	-	Ireland
Mary Mahony	Daughter	3	-	Swansea
+ 4 sons	-	7 - 15	-	Swansea
Thomas Mahony	Son	15	-	Swansea

Michael Row

David Dunovon	Head	40	Labourer Cork	
Eleanora Dunovan	Wife	24	-	Cork
Bridget Dunovan	Daughter	3 mths	-	Swansea
Thos. Finley	Lodger	32	Labourer	Cork
John Welsh	Lodger	22	Labourer	Waterford
Ann Welsh	Wife	21	-	Waterford
Mary Neal	Lodgr	28	Hawker	Waterford
Peter Dugan	Head	47	Labourer	Cork
Mary Dugan	Wife	30	-	Cork
+ 6 children	-	1 - 11	-	Cork
John Dunavon	Lodger	35	Labourer	Cork
Mary Dunavon	Wife	30	-	Cork
+ 2 daughters	-	5 & 9	-	Cork
Michael Long	Lodger	30	Labourer	Cork
Catharine Long	Wife	32	-	Cork
Eleanor Long	Daughter	12	-	Cork
Thomas Power	Head	30	Labourer	Ireland
Mary Power	Wife	30	-	Ireland
+ 2 daughters	-	2 & 9	-	Ireland
Patrick Dower	Lodger	40	Labourer	Ireland
James Connely	Lodger	35	Labourer	Ireland

Jeremiah Bryan	Head	40	Labourer	Ireland
Mary Bryan	Wife	30	-	Ireland
William	Son	5	-	Ireland
Daniel Collins	Lodger	30	Labourer	Ireland
Ann Collins	Wife	29	-	Ireland
Anthony Walsh	Lodger	28	Labourer	Ireland
Mary Walsh	Wife	24	-	Ireland
Jeremiah Cafrey	Lodger	30	Labourer	Ireland
Mary Cafrey	Wife	20	-	Ireland
Samel Sheen	Lodger	40	Fisherman	Ireland
Margaret Collins	Lodger	59	-	Ireland
Margaret Sheen	Head	46	-	Ireland
John Sheen	Son	14	-	Ireland
Patrick Sheen	Son	9	-	Ireland
Thos. Sheen	Son	4	-	Ireland
Mary Sheen	Daughter	13	-	Ireland
William Dolly	Lodger	50	Labourer	Ireland
Michael Dolly	Lodger	20	Labourer	Ireland
Nancy Green	Lodger	22	-	Ireland
Ellin Sillavin	Lodger	24	Servant	Ireland
Daniel Sillavin	Lodger	12	-	Ireland
Mary Erly	Lodger	25	-	Ireland
William Sandry	Head	54	Traveller	Ireland
Elizabeth Sandry	Wife	47	-	Ireland
Margaret Sandry	Daughter	11	-	Cardiff
Daniel Mahony	Head	26	Labourer	Ireland
Mary Mahony	Wife	28	-	Ireland
Margaret Mahony	Daughter	18 mths	-	Swansea
Cornelius McCarty	Lodger	40	Labourer	Ireland
Mary McCarty	Wife	20	-	Ireland
Margaret McCarty	Daughter	3 mths	-	Swansea
Paul Sheen	Lodger	30	Labourer	Ireland
Catherine Sheen	Wife	30	-	Ireland
+ 4 children	-	1 - 9	-	Ireland
Andrew Roerson	Head	29	Copperman	Ireland
Ann Roerson	Wife	27	-	Ireland
John Roerson	Son	7	School	Swansea
+ 2 sons	-	2 & 5	School	Swansea
Angel Street				
Richard Lynes	Lodger	35	Labourer	Ireland
Mary Lynes	Wife	30	-	Ireland
+ 3 children		-8 mths - 8 years	-	Ireland

John Roach	Head	40	Labourer	Ireland
Mary Roach	Wife	40	-	Ireland
Michael Roach	Son	10	-	Swansea
Daniel Clifford	Lodger	20	Labourer	Ireland
Daniel Sellaon	Lodger	60	Labourer	Ireland
James Healeie	Lodger	24	Labourer	Ireland
Michael Wasley	Head	50	Labourer	Ireland
Catharine Wasley	Wife	40	-	Ireland
+ 2 sons	-	14 & 17	Labourers	Ireland
Mary Wasley	Daughter	11	-	Swansea
+ 2 sons (John & James)	?	-	-	Swansea
Daniel Conolly	Head	38	Labourer	Ireland
Catherine Connolly	Wife	37	-	Ireland
Jeremiah Conolly	Son	15	Labourer	London
+ 2 daughters	-	10 & 12	-	London
Denis Connolly	Son	8	-	Bristol
John Connolly	Son	1	-	Swansea
James Cockly	Lodger	12	-	Cork
Honora Patterson	Lodger	69	-	Cork
Daniel Collins	Head	34	Labourer	Ireland
Hanora Collins	Wife	31	-	Ireland
Patrick Collins	Son	8	-	Ireland
Mary Henigan	Lodger	4	-	Swansea
Edward Corbert	Head	30	Labourer	Ireland
Rebeca Corbert	Wife	22	-	Ireland
Edward Corbert	Son	2	-	Swansea
Timothy Connor	Head	32	Labourer	Ireland
Ellin Connor	wife	24	-	Ireland
Michael Connor	Son	2	-	Ireland
Larins Brynen	Head	32	Labourer	Ireland
Mary Brynen	Wife	30	-	Ireland
+ 2 sons	-	4 & 9	-	Ireland
Eleanora Brynen	Daughter	11 mths	-	Swansea
Edmond Ryan	Head	40	Labourer	Ireland
Ann Ryan	Wife	35	-	Ireland
Edward Ryan	Son	13	Labourer	Ireland
Johanna Ryan	Daughter	3	-	Swansea
Thomas Ryan	Son	2 mths	-	Swansea
Llangyfelach Street				
Hannora William	Head	40	Let Lodgings	Ireland
Catharine William	Daughter	17	Servant	Ireland
Edward William	Son	14	Labourer	Ireland

Cornelius Logan	Lodger	18	Labourer	Ireland
Stephan Sellaven	Lodger	20	Labourer	Ireland
Jeremiah Mahoney	Head	60	Labourer	Ireland
Mary Mahoney	Wife	59	-	Ireland
+ 4 children	-	11 - 26	-	Ireland
Patrick Delaney	Lodger	40	Labourer	Ireland
Nancy Delaney	Wife	27	Servant	Ireland
Mary Connor	Lodger	60	-	Ireland
Mary Leary	Lodger	45	Dressmaker	Ireland
Johannah Deecey	Lodger	75	-	Ireland
Ellin Leary	Lodger	45	Dressmaker	Ireland
Edward Murphy	Head	44	Labourer	Ireland
Ellin Murphy	Wife	45	-	Ireland
John Murphy	Son	15	-	Ireland
Daniel Murphy	Son	9	-	Swansea
+ 2 sons	-	3 & 7	-	Swansea
John Dacey	Head	60	Labourer	Ireland
Elizabeth Dacey	Wife	61	-	Ireland
Thomas Dacey	Lodger	23	Labourer	Ireland
Patrick Roady	-	24	Labourer	Ireland
Mary Roady	Wife	20	-	Ireland
Robert Roady	Son	5 mths	-	Swansea
Ann Connoly	Head	50	Keeping Lodgers	Ireland
Ann Connoly	Daughter	22	Servant	Ireland
Jeremiah Connoly	Son	15	Sailor	Ireland
John Sillivan	Lodger	30	Labourer	Ireland
John Sillivan	Lodger	30	Labourer	Ireland
Richard Sillivan	Lodger	29	Labourer	Ireland
Patrick Sillivan	Lodger	22	Labourer	Ireland
Wiliam Fitzgerald	Head	37	Labourer	Ireland
Mary Fittzgerlad	Wife	30	-	Ireland
Johanna Fitzgerald	Daughter	10	-	Swansea
+ 3 children	-	1 - 8	-	Swansea
William Akins	Lodger	26	Labourer	Ireland
Daniel Brogan	Head	30	Labourer	Ireland
Ellin Brogan	Wife	30	-	Ireland
Nancy Brogan	Daughter	7	-	Swansea
+ 3 sons	-	1 mth - 6	-	Swansea
Jery Brayant	Lodger	26	Labourer	Ireland
Patrick Driscol	Lodger	25	Labourer	Ireland
Nancy Driscol	Lodger	22	-	Ireland
Mary Dunavon	Lodger	30	Labourer at the works	Ireland

Mary Colvene	Lodger	25	Labourer at the works	Ireland
Johanna Walch	Lodger	29	Labourer at the works	Ireland
William Taylor	Head	34	Labourer	Ireland
Ellin Taylor	Wife	32	-	Ireland
Thomas Taylor	Son	7	Labourer	Swansea
James Bowling	Lodger	20	Labourer	Ireland
Edward Cheers	Lodger	23	Labourer	Ireland
Edward Sexton	Lodger	22	Labourer	Ireland
Jeremiah Roche	Lodger	22	Labourer	Ireland
Samuel Sullivan	Lodger	27	Labourer	Ireland
Catherine Sullivan	Lodger	18	Dressmaker	Ireland
Thos. Casey	Lodger	22	Stone Mason	Ireland
Margaret Dun	Lodger	20	Labouring	Ireland
Margaret Ruset	Lodger	70	-	Ireland
Timothy Sillavan	Head	25	Labourer	Ireland
Johanna Sillivan	Wife	23	-	Ireland
John Sillivan	Son	3	-	Swansea
Daniel Sillivan	Son	2	-	Swansea
Timothy Stacy	Lodger	30	Labourer	Ireland
Mary Stacey	Wife	25	-	Ireland
Daniel Stacey	Son	2	-	Swansea
John Shee	Lodger	28	-	Ireland
Mary Shillavon	Lodger	28	Servant	Ireland
John Lenard	Head	52	Labouring	Ireland
Mary Lenard	Wife	32	-	Ireland
Timothy Johean	Lodger	31	Labouring	Ireland
Mary Johean	Lodger	42	-	Ireland
Edward Johean	Lodger	15	Labouring	Ireland
Con Coughlan	Lodger	25	Labouring	Ireland
John Farnlow	Lodger	20	Labouring	Ireland
William Cafrey	Lodger	14	Labouring	Ireland
Bridgit Brayan	Lodger	27	-	Ireland
Bridgit Collins	Lodger	19	-	Ireland
Jeremiah Sillaven	Head	60	Labourer	Ireland
Mary Sillaven	Wife	40	-	Ireland
Onora Sillaven	Daughter	13	-	Glamorganshire
Jeremiah Sillaven	Son	11	-	Swansea
John Sillaven	Son	8	-	Swansea
Jeremiah Leary	Lodger	21	-	Ireland
Elizabeth Leary	Lodger	15	-	Swansea
Margaret Solevane	Lodger	35	-	Ireland
Cornelius Lery	Head	40	Labourer	Ireland

Mary Lery	Wife	34	-	Ireland
+ 5 children	-	2 - 14	-	Ireland
John Dunavon	Lodger	36	Labourer	Ireland
Judy Dunavon	Wife	36	-	Ireland
Biddy Dunavon	Daughter	2	-	Ireland
John Sillavon	Head	30	Labourer	Ireland
Nancy Sillavon	Wife	27	-	Ireland
+ 2 daughters	-15 mths & 6 years-			Ireland
Mathew Green	Lodger	29	Labourer	Ireland
Julie Green	Wife	21	-	Ireland
John Green	Son	10 mths	-	Ireland
Catherine Driscol	-	26	-	Ireland
Pat Sullavon	-	23	Labourer	Ireland
Nicholas Walsh	Head	40	Shoemaker	Ireland
Sarah Walsh	Daughter	14	-	Swansea
Patrick Reley	-	56	Labourer	Ireland
Elizabeth Reley	Daughter	16	-	Ireland
Patrick Mahony	Head	45	Shoemaker	Ireland
Mary Mahony	Wife	35	-	Ireland
Patrick Sillavon	Head	49	Labourer	Ireland
Mary Sillavon	Daughter	10	-	Swansea
Denis Sillavon	Son	4	-	Swansea
Pontyglasdwr				
Daniel Chamoran	Head	40	Labourer	Ireland
Eleanora Chamoran	Wife	32	-	Ireland
+ 2 daughters	-	3 & 6	-	Ireland
John Chamoran	Son	9 mths	-	Swansea
John Keeffe	Lodger	71	Labourer	Ireland
John Keeffe	Lodger	18	Labourer	Ireland
Cornelius Kely	Lodger	14	Labourer	Ireland
Edward Alworth	Head	24	Labourer	Ireland
Mary Alworth	Wife	32	-	Ireland
Henry Alworth	Son	6	-	Ireland
Denis Brin	Lodger	20	Sailor	Ireland
Timothy Brin	Lodger	18	Sailor	Ireland
Patrick Sillavon	Lodger	30	Labourer	Ireland
Mary Green	Lodger	30	Housemaid	Ireland
Freda Mahony	Lodger	70	-	Ireland
Judi Sillavon	Lodger	23	Housemaid	Ireland
Daniel Alworth	Head	66	Labourer	Ireland
Mary Alworth	Wife	56	-	Ireland
John Alworth	Son	22	Labourer	Ireland

	+ 2 sons	-	15 & 16	Labourers	Ireland
	Elen Murphy	Lodger	50	-	Ireland
	Elen Murphy	Daughter	22	Labourer	Ireland
	Denise Sillavon	Lodger	22	Labourer	Ireland

Carmarthen Road

1	Patrick Doyle	Lodger	36	Railway Labourer	Dublin
	Mary Doyle	Wife	33	-	Lancashire
	Ellan Doyle	Daughter	10 months	-	Dublin
2	John Mulvany	Head	36	Railway Labourer	Banbridge, Co
	Susanna Mulvany	Daughter	8	-	Banridge, Co
	Edward Mulvany	Son	5	-	Banbridge, Co
	Mary Mulvany	Daughter	2	-	Llansamlet
22	Barnard Cain	Head	45	Railway Labourer	Armagh
	Catharine Cain	Wife	40	-	Galway
	Catharine Cain	Daughter	5	-	Bristol
	William Cain	Son	3	-	Newport
	James Connell	Lodger	42	Railway Labourer	Owmey (Omagh?)
	Frank Kirn	Lodger	40	Railway Labourer	Derry

Brynsyfi

Town Hill Farm

Elizabeth Mahony	Head	43	Farmer's Wife	Mumbles
Honora Mahony	Daughter	15	-	Swansea
+ 2 sons (Thomas & John)		1 & 8	-	Swansea
John Sheanen	-	27	Farm Servant	Ireland
Daniel Sheanen	-	14	Farm Servant	Ireland

Corner House (Near Waun Wen - Nant y Glasdwr & Carmarthen Road)

John Connelly	Head	45	Railway Labourer	Killesham, Ireland
Catherine Connelly	Wife	45	-	Killesham, Ireland
+ 7 childen	-	5 - 18	-	Killesham, Ireland
Patrick Gribbin	Head	69	Railway Labourer	Co. Down
Patrick Farrel	Lodger	21	-	Kildare

Townhill Cottage

John Slatary	Head	34	Agricultural Labourer	Dungarvon, Waterford
Sarah Slatary	Wife	28	Housemaid	Pembrokeshire
+ 2 daughters	-	9 mths & 2 years	-	Swansea
Daniel Sullivan	Visitor	56	Agricultural Labourer	Kilnamuch, Ireland

May Hill				
Daniel Sullivan	Servant	50	Farm Servant	Kilnamuck
Sketty				
Red Lion				
John Burk	Head	32	Victualar	Ireland
Mary Burk	Wife	30	-	Oystermouth
+ 4 children	-	1 - 8	-	Swansea
Ferryside				
Jeffrey Sullivan	Head	49	Labourer	Ireland
Ellen Sullivan	Wife	42	-	Ireland
+ 4 children	-	12 - 21	-	Ireland
Jeremiah Harrington	Cousin	22	Tailor	Ireland
Dennis Mahony	Head	31	Labourer	Ireland
Jane Mahony	Wife	31	-	Swansea
Mary Mahony	Daughter	5	-	St Thomas, Swansea
+ 2 children	-	1 & 3	-	St Thomas, Swansea
Joannah Purcel	Head	51	-	Ireland
John Purcel	Son	18	Blacksmith	Swansea
Elizabeth Purcel	Daughter	14	-	Swansea

Appendix 3

The Census of 1861

	Name	Relation	Age	Occupation	Birthplace
Alma Terrace					
3	Thomas McKevitt	Head	40	Hawker in Drapery	Ireland
	Catherine McKevitt	Wife	38	-	Ireland
	Mary A McKevitt	Daughter	14	Scholar	Ireland
	John McKevitt	Son	12	Scholar	Ireland
	Bridget McKevitt	Daughter	10	-	Wrexham
	+ 2 children	-	6 & 8	-	Wrexham
	Thomas McKevitt	Son	3	-	Ireland (Haverfordwest)
	Michael McKevitt	Son	6 mths	-	Haverfordwest
	Mary A Nicholson	Head	50	Miliner	Ireland
	Mary A Nicholson	Daughter	15	-	Newborough, Anglesey
	Michael Furlong	Head	40	Cartman	Ireland
	Mary Furlong	Wife	39	-	Ireland
	+ 4 children	-	8 - 16	-	Ireland
	Eliza Furlong	Daughter	6	-	Swansea
	+ 2 children	-	2 & 4	-	Swansea
	Edward Kavanagh	B-in-law	36	Excavator	Ireland
Evans Row					
4	James Lynch	Lodger	35	Mariner	Ireland
	Mary Lynch	Lodger	31	-	Ireland
	James Forester	Head	49	Optician	Ireland
	Ellen Forester	Wife	49	-	Ireland
13	Johanna McDonna	Head	40	Sailor's widow	Ireland
	William McDonna	Son	5	-	Ireland
	Johanna McDonna	Daughter	2	-	Ireland
	Thomas Shelley	Head	39	Carriage Fitter	Ireland
	Ellen Shelley	Wife	36	-	Ireland
	+ 2 daughters	-	11 & 13	-	London
	+ 2 sons	-	7 & 9	-	Birmingham
	James Shelley	-	4	-	Swansea
Williams Place					
1	Dennis Madden	Head	42	General Labourer	Ireland
	Mary Madden	Wife	45	-	Ireland
	Henry Radley	Lodger	72	Pensioner	Ireland
	John Holoran	Head	50	Shoemaker	Ireland

	Mary Holoran	Wife	40	-	Ireland
2	Michael O'Neill	Head	33	General Labourer	Ireland
	Catherine O'Neill	Wife	30	-	Ireland
	Mary O'Neill	Daughter	2	-	Swansea
Dyfatty Street					
11	Golden Lion				
	George Harvey				
12	William Sullivan	Head	32	General Labourer	Ireland
	Mary Sullivan	Wife	30	-	Ireland
	David Power	Lodger	26	General Labourer	Ireland
	+ Morgan Family x 5				
38	John Quinn	Head	36	General Labourer	Ireland
	Bridgett Quinn	Wife	40	-	Ireland
	+ 2 sons	-	5 & 10	-	Ireland
	Bridgett Quinn	Daughter	3	-	Swansea
	Ellen Burns	Orphan	15	General Servant	Swansea
Flint Row (Strand)					
1	Ann Corkran	Head(W)	60	Charwoman	Cork
	Jane Corkran	Daughter	22	-	Swansea
	+ 2				
2	Jeremiah Murphy	Head	37	Labourer	Cork
	Ellen Murphy	Wife	35	-	Kinmare
	Patrick Murphy	Son	3	-	Swansea
	John Barry	Head	35	-	Bandon
	Mary Barry	-	30	-	Bandon
	+ 2 sons	-	4 & 7	-	Swansea
3	Timothy Sullivan	Head	58	Marine Store Dealer	Skebereen
	Mary Sullivan	Wife	44	-	Co. Kerry
	Mary Bowland	Boarder	69	Charwoman	Dungarvan
	Dinnis Bowland	Son	40	Labourer	Dungarvan
Old Gate House Cottages					
4	Michael Bride	Head	45	Labourer	Cork
	Johanna Bride	Wife	29	-	Tipperary
	+ 2 sons	-	1 & 5	-	Swansea
	Daniel White	Boarder	34	Labourer	Cork
	Jane White	Wife	25	-	Swansea
	John White	Son	6 mths	-	Swansea
Pottery Street					
9	William Mahony	Head	30	Labourer	Waterford
	Julia Mahony	Wife	40	-	Tipperary
Powell Street					
34	John Hart	Head	40	Chelsea Pensioner	Dublin

	Bridget Hart	Daughter	12	Scholar	Swansea
33	William Lucas	Head	45	Mariner	Dungarvan, Co. Waterford
	Mary Lucas	Wife	37	-	Cardiff
Jockey Street					
2	John Barrett	Head	32	Mason	Galway
	Ann Barrett	Wife	31	-	Mayho
	+ 3 children	-	1 - 9	-	Swansea
Jockey Court					
1	James Halpin	Head	38	Shoemaker	Dublin
	Julia Halpin	Wife	32	-	Dublin
	+ 4 children	-	1 - 9	-	Swansea
Matthew Street					
4	George Overend	Head	33	House Carpenter	Ireland
	Ann Overend	Wife	35	-	Ireland
	+ 2 children	-	6 & 9	-	Ireland
	Margaret Overend	Daughter	1	-	Cardiff
Bethesda Street					
17	Alexander Mahony	Head	35	Labourer	Tipperary
	June Mahony	Wife	30	-	Swansea
	+ 4 children	-	1 - 7	-	Swansea
St John Street					
4	Samuel McCarr	Head	34	Railway Porter	Co. Down
	Agnes McCarr	Wife	34	-	Gloster
	Issabella McCarr	Daughter	8	Scholar	Co. Clare
	Ann Jane McCarr	Daughter	6	-	Malta
	Eliza McCarr	Daughter	1	-	Swansea
18	Michael Leary	Head	35	Labourer	Ireland
	Ann Leary	Wife	30	-	Swansea
	+ 3 children	-	1 - 10	-	Swansea
19	Mary O'Brien	Head	49	Laundress	Ireland
	+ 3 children	-	11 - 17	-	Lancashire
23	Michael Reardon	Head	40	Shoemaker	Cork
	Catherine Reardon	Wife	40	Shoemaker Apprentice	Cork
	Michael Reardon	Son	16	Shoemaker Apprentice	Cork
	Mary Reardon	Daughter	14	Apprentice Pottery Printer	Bridgend
	+ 4 children	-	2,4,7 & 10	Scholars	Swansea
24	John Appleyard	Head	42	Labourer	Ireland
	Mary Appleyard	Wife	38	-	Ireland

	Name	Relation	Age	Occupation	Birthplace
	Patrick Appleyard	Son	13	-	Bristol
	+ 4 children	-	1 - 10	-	Swansea
Elephant Street					
3	Patrick Sullivan	Head	40	Labourer	Ireland
	Catharine Sullivan	Wife	30	-	Ireland
	+ 3 children		-5 mths - 4 years		Swansea
Chapel Street					
1	John Doyle	Head	28	Labourer	Ireland
	Catharine Doyle	Wife	21	-	Ireland
	Bridget Kieth	-	17	Servant (Outdoors)	Ireland
Green Row					
3b	John Callahan	Head	50	Labourer	Ireland
	Catharine Callahan	Wife	40	-	Ireland
	Bridget Callahan	Daughter	19	Fruit Dealer	Birkenhead
	Jefery Callahan	Son	16	Labourer	Monmouthshire
	May A Callahan	Daughter	14	Scholar	Dowlais
	Catharine Callahan	Daughter	12	Scholar	Swansea
	+ 3 children	-	6 - 9	Scholars	Swansea
2	Paul Aherne	Head	40	Labourer	Ireland
	Catharine Aherne	Wife	40	-	Ireland
	Patrick Aherne	Son	14	Labourer	Ireland
	Thomas Aherne	Son	10	Labourer	Ireland
	Catherine Dacy	Widow	50	-	Ireland
	Nicholas Dacy	Son	17	Labourer	Swansea
Green Row (Court)					
1	Michael Shannon	Head	37	Labourer	Ireland
	Ann Shannon	Wife	50	-	Glamorgan
	Ellen Shannon	Daughter	17	At home	Ireland
	Daniel Shannon	Son	16	Blacksmith	Swansea
	Patrick Ataher	Head	45	Labourer	Ireland
	+ 3 children	-	12 - 18	-	Ireland
	James Ataher	Son	4	-	Swansea
Greenhill Court					
	Thomas F Gwinn	Head	35	Shoemaker	Ireland
	Mary Gwinn	Wife	27	-	Ireland
	+ 2 children	-	2 & 4	-	Swansea
	MaryLayns	Lodger	35	Laundress	Ireland
	Mary Layns	Daughter	2	-	Merthyr
1	Timothy Donovan	Head	50	Labourer	Ireland
	Hanorah Donovan	Wife	40	-	Ireland
	+ 2 children	-	12 & 16	-	Ireland
	John Downey	Lodger	24	-	Ireland

	Name	Relation	Age	Occupation	Birthplace
	Mary Downey	Wife	26	-	Ireland
	Daniel Downey	Son	1	-	Swansea
	Daniel Lacy	Head	30	Labourer	Ireland
	Catharine Lacy	Wife	32	-	Ireland
	+ 5 children	-8 mths - 11 years-			Swansea
Greenhill Street					
4	Patrick Rimnum	Head	33	Shoemaker	Ireland
	MargaretRimnum	Wife	30	-	Ireland
	William Rimnum	Son	14	Labourer	Ireland
	+ 4 children	-	1 - 11	-	Swansea
5	Cornelius O'Brien	Head	25	Labourer	Ireland
	Ellen O'Brien	Wife	20	-	Ireland
	Mary O'Brien	Daughter	2	-	Greenhill
	John O'Brien	Son	4 mths	-	Greenhill
	Ellen Lane	Boarder	30	-	Ireland
	Ellen Griffiths	Boarder	26	Servant	Ireland
6	John Renehan	Head	50	Labourer	Ireland
	Ann Renehan	Wife	44	-	Ireland
	Hanorah Renehan	Daughter	17	-	Ireland
	William Renehan	Son	24	Labourer	Ireland
1	Timothy Donovan	Head	50	Labourer	Ireland
	Hanorah Donovan	Wife	40	-	Ireland
	+ 2 children	-	12 & 16	-	Ireland
	John Downey	Lodger	24	Labourer	Ireland
	Mary Downey	Wife	26	_	Ireland
	Daniel Downey	Son	1	-	Swansea
	Daniel Lacy	Head	30	Labourer	Ireland
	Catharine Lacy	Wife	32	-	Ireland
	+ 5 children	-8 mths - 11 years-			Swansea
4	Dennis Murphy	Head	46	Labourer	Ireland
	Elina Murphy	Wife	43	-	Ireland
	+ 4 children	-	3 - 14	-	Swansea
	John Rawe	Boarder	63	Labourer	Ireland
	Daniel Callahan	Lodger	50	Labourer	Swansea
	John Fitzpatrick	Lodger	60	Labourer	Swansea
	John Cain	Lodger	17	Labourer	Swansea
	Michael Hannen	Lodger	45	Labourer	Ireland
	Catharine Callahan	-	40	Wife of Labourer	Ireland
9	Joseph Woods	Lodger	40	Hawker	Ireland
	Margaret Woods	Wife	37	-	Ireland
	Margaret Woods	Daughter	18	-	Ramsgate, Kent
	Ellen Leary	Lodger	21	Washerwoman	Newport

10	Thomas Enright	Head	58	Labourer	Ireland
	Ellen Enright	Daughter	20	Servant	Swansea
	George Enright	Son	17	Sailor	Swansea
	Michael Brien	Lodger	47	Hawker	Ireland
	Susan Brien	Wife	35	-	Ireland
	+ 2 children	-	3 & 5	-	Pembroke
11	John Harrington	Head	28	Labourer	Ireland
	Catherine Harrington	Wife	27	-	Ireland
	May Harrington	Daughter	8	-	Merthyr Tydfil
	Catherine Harrington	Daughter	6	-	Merthyr Tydfil
	Bridget Harrington	Daughter	6	-	Merthyr Tydfil
	Anora Harrington	Daughter	2 mths	-	Swansea
	Mary Murray	Lodger	26	Outdoor Servant	Ireland
12	Dennis Doyle	Head	33	Labourer	Ireland
	Elizabeth Doyle	Wife	38	-	Narberth
	+ 3 children	-	7 - 11	-	Neath
	Catherine Doyle	Daughter	15 mths	-	Swansea
18	Timothy Murphy	Head	26	Labourer	Ireland
	Margaret Murphy	Wife	24	-	Ireland
	+ 2 children	-	1 mth & 2 years		Swansea
27	Patrick Daly	Head	33	Engine Driver	Ireland
	Charlotte M Daly	Wife	25	Dressmaker	Swansea
	+ 2 children	-	1 & 3	-	Swansea
32	John Flyn	Head	36	Labourer	Ireland
	Mary Flyn	Wife	34	-	Ireland
	Patrick Kating	Head	21	Smelter	Ireland
	Sarah Kating	Wife	20	_	Swansea
	Johannah Kating	Daughter	6 mths	-	Swansea
34	William Kennedy	Head	26	Shoemaker	Ireland
	Ann Kennedy	Wife	25	-	Ireland
	Thomas Kennedy	Son	3	-	Swansea
	Johannah Cotter	S-in-law	15	-	Ireland
44	Maurice Conor	Head	34	Labourer	Ireland
	Margaret Conor	Wife	35	-	Ireland
	Mary Conor	Daughter	6	-	Aberdare
	Ellen Conor	Daughter	4	-	Swansea
	William Conor	Son	2	-	Swansea
East Place					
3	Thomas Joy	Head	30	Labourer	Ireland
	Ellen Joy	Wife	30	Labourer	Ireland
	James Aherne	Wife's Son	14	Labourer	Ireland
	Patrick Joy	Son	11	Scholar	Ireland

	Name	Relation	Age	Occupation	Birthplace
	+ 3 children	-	5 - 9	Scholars	Ireland
Coomb Street					
2	Thomas O'Hara	Head	58	Labourer & Publican	Ireland
Pub	Mary O'Hara	Wife	50	_	Ireland
	Michael O'Hara	Son	12	Scholar	Swansea
	Roger Sheen	Lodger	45	Labourer	Ireland
	John McCarty	Lodger	32	Labourer	Ireland
	Mary McCarty	Wife	22	-	Ireland
	Mary McCarty	Daughter	2 weeks	-	Swansea
	Margaret Carty	Head	58	Seamstress	Ireland
	James Burns	Grandson	17	Labourer	Swansea
	John Donovan	Head	32	Farmer of 30 acres	Ireland
	Johannah Donovan	Wife	29	-	Ireland
	Julia Donovan	Daughter	6	-	Merthyr
	James Donovan	Son	3	-	Maesteg
	Jerry Murphy	Lodger	24	Labourer	Ireland
	Patrick Kennly	Lodger	20	Labourer	Ireland
4	Ann Sulivan	Head (W)	60	Lodging House Keeper	Ireland
	Cornelius Sulivan	Son	34	Labourer	Ireland
	Mary Hoare	Lodger	32	Sailor's Wife	Ireland
	John Hoare	Son	7	-	Swansea
	Patrick Murphy	Lodger	23	Labourer	Ireland
	Mary Murphy	Wife	20	-	Ireland
	Patrick Murphy	Son	2	-	Ireland
	Michael Murphy	Son	2 mths	-	Swansea
	Mary Leary	Lodger	30	-	Ireland
	Margaret Leary	Daughter	3	-	Swansea
	Mary Hore	Daughter of Lodger	9	-	Swansea
5	John Barry	Head	41	Labourer	Ireland
	Mary Barry	Wife	35	-	Ireland
	Sarah Mulcahy	Step Daughter	11	Scholar	Shropshire
	Ellen Barry	Daughter	8	Scholar	Shropshire
	Bridget Barry	Daughter	4	-	Swansea
	Catharine Barry	Daughter	1	-	Swansea
	William Wilaw	Head	53	Labourer	Ireland
	Mary Wilaw	Wife	35	-	Ireland
	John Wilaw	Son	22	Coach Smith	Ireland
	+ 4 children	-	14 - 20	-	Ireland
6	John Sulivan	Head	30	Labourer	Ireland
	Ann Sulivan	Wife	30	-	Ireland

	Name	Relation	Age	Occupation	Birthplace
	Honorah Sulivan	Head	36	Lodging House Keeper	Ireland
	Daniel Sulivan	Son	9	Scholar	Swansea
	+ 2 children	-	3 & 6	-	Swansea
	Daniel Sulivan	Lodger	70	Labourer	Ireland
	William Conor	Visitor	48	Fiddler	Ireland
7	John Mahony	Head	40	Labourer	Ireland
	Cathrine Mahony	Wife	30	-	Ireland
	Patrick Mahony	Son	41/2	-	Swansea
	+ 2 children		-16 mths & 3 years-		Swansea
	Patrick Sulivan	Head	55	Labourer	Ireland
	Honora Sulivan	Wife	50	-	Ireland
	Mary Sulivan	Daughter	6	Scholar	Swansea
	+ 2 daughters	-	3 & 5	Scholars	Swansea
	John Harrington	Lodger	21	Labourer	Ireland
	Cornelius Neil	Lodger	21	Labourer	Ireland
8	Patrick Vale	Head	26	Labourer	Ireland
	Margaret Vale	Wife	23	-	Ireland
	Dennis Shee	Head	24	Copperman	Ireland
	Margaret Shee	Wife	23	-	Ireland
	Margaret Shee	Daughter	9	-	Ireland
	Patrick Hogan	Lodger	23	Copperman	Ireland
	Patrick Lowney	Lodger	21	Copperman	Ireland
	Edmond Tobin	Head	24	Copperman	Ireland
	Magaret Tobin	Wife	23	-	Ireland
	Alice Tobin	Widow	55	-	Ireland
9	Patrick O'Brien	Head	53	Labourer	Ireland
	Hanorah O'Brien	Wife	35	-	Ireland
	Dan'l Shannon	Head	80	Labourer	Ireland
	Margaret Shannon	Wife	92	-	Ireland
	Bridget O'Brien	Daughter	7	-	Swansea
	Margaret Ponsonby	Head	50	Widow/Pauper	Ireland
King's Head					
10	Patrick Fitzgerald	Head	40	Publican	Ireland
	Johannah Fitzgerald	Wife	32	-	Ireland
	Catharine Fitzgerald	Daughter	10	Scholar	Oystermouth
	Joseph Fitzgerald	Son	17	Scholar	Swansea
	+ 2 children	-	3 & 5	-	Swansea
	Daniel Shaw	Boarder	28	Labourer	Ireland
	Michael Walsh	Lodger	26	Labourer	Ireland
Greenfield Street					
1	James McCarley	Head	32	Cabinet Maker	Ireland

	Catherine McCarley	Wife	30	-	Ireland
	+ 3 children	-	8 - 14	-	Manchester
	+ 2 children	-	3 & 6	-	Liverpool
10	Thomas Dolling	Head	41	Plumber	Limerick
	Catherine Dolling	Wife	27	-	Prescot, Lancs.
	William H Dolling	Son	3	-	Liverpool
	+ 2 children	-	2 mths & 1 year	-	Swansea
Inkerman Street					
19	William Linehan	Head	40	Railway Porter	Ireland
	Margaret Linehan	Wife	40	-	Ireland
	+ 4 children	-	8 - 15	-	Bath
	+ 2 sons	-	5 & 8	-	Neath
Green Row					
	James Conoly	Head	40	Labourer	Ireland
	Sarah Conoly	Wife	40	-	Ireland
	Ann Conoly	Daughter	14	-	Ireland
	James Conoly	Son	10	-	Chester
	John Conoly	Son	8	-	Lancashire
	Jane Conoly	Daughter	5	-	Swansea
Brook Street					
2	Timothy Barnet	Head	50	Labourer	Ireland
	Mary Barnet	Wife	45	-	Ireland
	+ 3 sons	-	7 - 12	-	Swansea
5	James Stuart	Head	32	Labourer	Ireland
	Margaret Stuart	-	33	-	Carmarthen
	William Stuart	Son	10	-	Ireland
	Sarah Stuart	Daughter	71/2	-	Carmarthen
	Mary Ann Stuart	Daughter	11	-	Carmarthen
	James Stuart	Son	1	-	Neath
	Maurice Mahony	Head	26	Copperman	Ireland
	Hanora Mahony	Wife	22	-	Ireland
6	Thomas Bowen	Head	47	Labourer	Ireland
	Bridget Bowen	Wife	35	-	Ireland
	+ 2 sons	-	11 - 14	-	Ireland
	Mary Shee	Visitor	6	-	Glamorganshire
	John Gogin	Head	48	Labourer	Ireland
	Mary Gogin	Wife	50	-	Ireland
	Patrick Huset	Lodger	35	Labourer	Ireland
	Johannah Huset	Wife	32	-	Ireland
	Patrick Huset	Son	1 mth	-	Swansea
7	Joseph Grady	Head	40	Copperman	Ireland
	Mary Grady	Wife	24	-	Ireland

	Johannah Grady	Daughter	3	-	Cardiff
	Ellen Grady	Daughter	4 mths	-	Swansea
	Michael Fleming	Head	48	Copperman	Ireland
	Ellen Fleming	Wife	30	-	Ireland
	+ 2 daughters	-	7 & 9	-	Ireland
	+ 3 children		-6 mths - 5 years	-	Swansea
	Patrick Powell	Lodger	18	Copperman	Ireland
	William Molloney	Lodger	23	Copperman	Ireland
	Morris Lane	Lodger	20	Copperman	Ireland
	Catharine Powell	Lodger	21	Pottery Girl	Ireland
8	John Donovan	Head	40	Labourer	Ireland
	Ellen Donovan	Wife	40	-	Ireland
	+ 3 daughters	-	7 - 12	-	Ireland
	Bridget Donovan	Daughter	6	-	Swansea
9	John Byard	Head	30	Shoemaker	Ireland
	Ellen Byard	Wife	27	-	Ireland
	+ 2 children	-	2 & 4	-	Merthyr
	Mary Byard	Daughter	4 mths	-	Swansea
	John Nail	Head	36	Labourer	Ireland
	Ellen Nail	Wife	35	-	London
	+ 3 children		-8 mths - 1 year	-	Swansea
10	Lawrence Sway	Head	30	Collier	Ireland
	Margaret Sway	Wife	29	-	Ireland
	+ 3 children	-	3 - 8	-	Wales (n.k.)
	Margaret Sway	Daughter	4 mths	-	Swansea
	Bridget?	Lodger	28	Washerwoman	Ireland
	Ellen Bower	Lodger	22	Pottery Girl	Ireland
	Catharine Murphy	Lodger	28	Pottery Girl	Ireland
	Alley Fitzgerald	Lodger	17	Pottery Girl	Ireland
	Ellen Murphy	Lodger	3	-	Swansea
11	Timothy Connors	Head	42	Labourer (Coke Yard)	Ireland
	Ellen Connors	Wife	34	-	Ireland
	Michael Conners	Son	13	-	Ireland
	+ 4 sons	-	1 - 91	-	Swansea
	Lawrence Shea	Lodger	20	Copperman	Ireland
	William Malloney	Lodger	30	Copperman	Ireland
	John Murray	Lodger	30	Copperman	Ireland
	Richard O'Brien	Head	25	Labourer (Patent Fuel Company)	Ireland
	Hannah O'Brien	Wife	24	-	Ireland
	May O'Brien	Daughter	3	-	Swansea

	Michael O'Brien	Son	2	-	Swansea
12	John Roach	Head	42	Copperman	Ireland
	Mary Roach	Wife	49	-	Ireland
	Michael Roach	Son	18	Clerk (Telegraph)	Swansea
13	Michael Sulivan	Head	28	Mariner	Ireland
	Catharine Sulivan	Wife	25	-	Ireland
	Edward Sulivan	Son	2½	-	Swansea
	Edward Fitzgerald	Head	60	Labourer	Ireland
	Mary Fitzgerald	Wife	45	-	Ireland
	James Fitzgerald	Son	17	Labourer	Ireland
	Mary Ann Fitzgerald	Daughter	15	Scholar	Ireland
	Ellen Fitzgerald	Visitor	21	Waitress	Ireland
14	John Dorney	Head	40	Copperman	Ireland
	Mary Dorney	Wife	35	-	Ireland
	John Dorney	Son	10	Scholar	Ireland
	Catharine Dorney	Daughter	7	-	Ireland
	James Dorney	Son	5	-	Swansea
	+ 2 children		-5 mths & 3 years	-	Swansea
	Michael Donovan	Lodger	36	Labourer	Ireland
15	Daniel Sulivan	Head	27	Labourer	Ireland
	Elizabeth Sulivan	Wife	27	-	Ireland
	Dennis Sulivan	Son	2	-	Aberavon
	Hanora Sulivan	Daughter	10 mths	-	Swansea
	Patrick Early	Head	28	Labourer	Ireland
	Margaret Early	Wife	30	-	Ireland
	John Early	Son	7	Scholar	Ireland
	Thomas Early	Son	5	-	Cardiff
	Patrick Early	Son	2	-	Swansea
	James Early	Son	9 mths	-	Swansea
16	Jeremiah Lynch	Head	26	Labourer	Ireland
	Margaret Lynch	Wife	25	-	Ireland
	Jeremiah Lynch	Son	2	-	Swansea
	+ 2 children	-	4 & 1	-	Swansea
	Mary Vay	Lodger	21	Outdoor Domestic Srvt	Ireland
	Ellen Pour	Lodger	21	Outdoor Domestic Srvt	Ireland
	Hannah Pour	Lodger	21	Outdoor Domestic Srvt	Ireland
17	Thomas Walsh	Head	40	Copperman	Ireland
	Margaret Walsh	Wife	23	-	Ireland
	Mary Kief	S-in-law	30	-	Ireland

	Patrick Kief	B-in-law	24	Labourer	Ireland
	Michael Walsh	Son	4	-	Swansea
	Kate Walsh	Daughter	2	-	Swansea
18	Michael Norman	Head	35	Labourer	Ireland
	Catherine Norman	Wife	30	-	Ireland
	Patrick Norman	Son	17	Scholar	Swansea
	+ 2 children	-	5 & 2	-	Swansea
	John Connor	Head	30	Labourer	Ireland
	Hannah Connor	Wife	30	-	Ireland
	Mary Connor	Daughter	3	-	Swansea
	John Connor	Son	2	-	Swansea
19	John Sweeny	Head	30	Labourer	Ireland
	Jemimah Sweeny	Wife	24	-	Ireland
	Margaret Sweeny	Daughter	4	-	Swansea
	+ 2 sons - 3 months & 2 years		-	Swansea	
	Michael Walsh	Head	28	Labourer	Ireland
	Bridget Walsh	Wife	30	-	Ireland
	+ 2 children	-5 months & 3 years			- Swansea
20	Thomas Hanniny	Head	23	Labourer	Ireland
	Ann Hanniny	Wife	23	-	Ireland
	John Hanniny	Son	7	-	Swansea
	Edmund Welch	Head	31	Copperman	Ireland
	Mary Welch	Wife	32	-	Ireland
	James Welch	Son	7	-	Swansea
	Patrick Welch	Son	7	-	Swansea
	+ 2 children	-	1 & 2	-	Swansea
Croft Street					
5	Jeremiah McCarty	Head	38	Labourer	Ireland
	Esther McCarty	Wife	38	-	Cardiganshire
	Mary McCarty	Daughter	8	Scholar	Mumbles
	+ 3 children	-	1 - 6	-	Mumbles
	Charles McCarty	Brother	25	Taylor	Ireland
	Bridgit McCarty	Mother	74	-	Ireland
	Michael Croke	Lodger	36	Labourer	Ireland
7	Denis Burns	Head	58	Labourer	Ireland
	Janet Burns	Wife	40	-	Ireland
	John Burns	Son	19	Clerk	Swansea
	Denis Burns	Son	17	Joiner	Swansea
12	James Connel	Head	48	Labourer	Ireland
	Anna Connel	Wife	49	-	Swansea
	Anna F Connel	Daughter	12	Scholar	Swansea
18	John Linnard	Head	40	Labourer	Ireland

	May Linnard	Wife	42	-	Ireland
	Bridget Linnard	Daughter	10	Scholar	Swansea
	Ann Ryne	Lodger	20	-	Ireland
	John Ryne	Lodger	29	Labourer	Ireland
21	Patrick Rhine	Head	40	Labourer	Ireland
	Bridget Rhine	Wife	37	-	Ireland
	Ann Rhine	Daughter	16	-	Ireland
	John Rhine	Son	9	-	Swansea
	+ 2 daughters	-	1 & 4	-	Swansea
23	Dan Conner	Head	32	Carter	Ireland
	Mary Conner	Wife	28	-	Puncheston, Pembroke
	Joseph Connor	Son	5	-	Prendergast, Pembroke
	Sarah Conner	Daughter	3	-	Swansea
	Thomas Conner	Son	1	-	Swansea
	John Smith	Lodger	32	Labourer	Ireland
	James Leigh	Lodger	23	Labourer	Ireland
Green Row (Cont . . .)					
1	John Heine	Head	35	Labourer	Ireland
	Margaret Heine	Wife	35	-	Ireland
	Patrick Heine	Son	8	-	Swansea
	+ 3 children		-5 mths - 7 years	-	Swansea
2	Thomas Meres	Head	32	Labourer	Ireland
	Catharine Meres	Wife	22	-	Ireland
	Mary Meres	Daughter	1	-	Swansea
5	Owen Keef	Head	27	Labourer	Ireland
	Ellen Keef	Wife	30	-	Ireland
	Patrick Keef	Son	3	-	Swansea
	+ 3 daughters		-1 month - 6 years	-	Swansea
6	John Power	Head	37	Labourer	Ireland
	Ellen Power	Wife	27	-	Ireland
	Thomas Power	Son 2 months		-	Swansea
High Street					
123	Mary McCarty	Head(W)	61	-	Ireland
	Patrick McCarty	Son	24	Grocer	Pembroke
	Anne McCarty	D-in-law	52	–	Essex
130	Maurice Duggan	Head	64	Shopkeepr & General Dealer	Ireland
	Elizabeth Duggan	Wife	50	-	Ireland
	Johannah Duggan	Daughter	18	-	Cardiff
	Mary Joyce	G. child	4	-	Neath

	William Carthy	Boarder	50	Workman	Ireland
131	Edmund Keating	Head	45	Furnaceman, Copperworks	Ireland
	Anne Keating	Wife	43	Grocer	Ireland
	Richerd Keating	Son	8	Scholar	Swansea
133	Daniel Gearin	Head	40	Land Surveyor	Ireland
	Mary Gearin	Wife	28	Housekeeper	Ireland
	Catharine Mahony	M-in-law	51	Housekeeper	Ireland
	Thomas Mahony	B-in-law	23	Labourer	Ireland
	Michael Mahony	B-in-law	19	Labourer	Ireland
134	Catharine Hickey	Head	51	Former Shopkeeper	Ireland
	Thomas Hickey	Son	23	Tailor	Ireland
	James Hickey	Son	22	Labourer	Ireland
135	William Gunnicliff	Head	36	Fishmonger	Tenby
	Julia Gunnicliff	Wife	30	-	Ireland
	Margaret Collins	M-in-law	60	-	Ireland
	John Mahony	Boarder	28	Labourer	Ireland
	Thomas Fitzgerald	Boarder	26	Labourer	Ireland
	Bridget Griffin	Lodger	30	Toy Seller	Ireland
	Thomas Tracy	Lodger	55	Shoemaker	Ireland
	James Rine	Lodger	40	Labourer	Ireland
	Catharine Lane	Lodger	50	General Servant	Ireland
136	Margaret McGrath	Head (W)	70	-	Ireland
	John McGrath	Son	30	Labourer	Ireland
	Thomas McGrath	Son	24	Labourer	Ireland
	Bridget McGrath	Daughter	20	Dressmaker	Ireland
	Catharine McGrath	Daughter	18	Dressmaker	Ireland
	Michael Murray	Grandson	4	-	Swansea
Margaret Court					
1	Thomas Flinn	Head	45	Coal Seller	Ireland
	Judy Flinn	Wife	46	-	Ireland
	Jane Leary	Boarder	20	Toy Seller	Ireland
3	Michael Marrney	Head	36	Furnaceman Copperworks	Ireland
	Bridgit Marrney	Wife	40	-	Ireland
	Michael Marrney	Son	11	-	Ireland
	Catherine Marrney	Daughter	7	-	Swansea
	Mary Terton	M-in-law	60	-	Ireland
	John Carrich	Boarder	38	Labourer	Ireland
Salutation or Lewis Court					
1	Thomas Joyce	Head	36	Labourer	Ireland
	Bridgit Joyce	Wife	27	-	Newport

	+ 2 daughters	-	11 & 16	-	Newport
3	Mary Collins	Head	50	House Keeper	Ireland
	Mary Collins	Daughter	18	Servant	Bristol
	Margaret Collins	Daughter	16	Servant	Bristol
	Maria Macklear	Lodger/Widow	-	Toy Seller, etc	London
	Ann Macklear	Daughter	16	Selling Coal	Swansea
	Alice Macklear	Daughter	7	-	Swansea
4	Mary Green	Head	50	-	Ireland
	Catharine Green	Daughter	15	-	Ireland
	Margaret Harrington	Boarder	50	-	Ireland
	+ 1 daughter	Boarder	9	-	Ireland
	Catharine Murphy	Boarder	22	General Servant	Ireland
	Johanna Murphy	Boarder	20	General Servant	Ireland
5	Mary Gravouth	Head	43	-	Ireland
	Edward Foren	S-in-law	23	Furnaceman	Ireland
	Margaret Foren	Daughter	19	-	Ireland

Greyhound Street

3	Thomas Walsh	Head	35	Labourer	Ireland
	Mary Walsh	Wife	32	-	Ireland
	Thomas Walsh	Son	2	-	Swansea
5	John Kelleher	Head	61	Labourer	Ireland
	Richard Kelleher	Son	26	Labourer	Ireland
	+ 3 children	-	16 - 22	-	Ireland
6	Jeremiah Spalane	Head	40	Labourer	Ireland
	Ellen Spalane	Wife	24	-	Ireland
	Mary Spalane	Daughter	14	-	Swansea
	John Merigan	Head	63	Labourer	Ireland
	Mary Merigan	Wife	24	-	Ireland
	John Merigan	Son	2	-	Ireland
	James Merigan	Son	6 mths	-	Swansea
8	Lawrence Murphy	Head	26	Labourer	Ireland
	Jane Murphy	Wife	21	-	Swansea
	Thomas Murphy	Son	15 mths	-	Swansea
12	James Heeley	Head	27	Labourer	London
	Catharine Heeley	Wife	27	-	Ireland
	James Heeley	Son	5	-	Swansea
	+ 3 children		-4 days - 4 years	-	Swansea
13	Edward McCarty	Head	36	Shoemaker	Ireland
	Margaret McCarty	Wife	30	-	Ireland
	John McCarty	Son	10	Apprentice Shoemaker	Ireland
	Julia McCarty	Daughter	8	Scholar	Ireland

	Mary Ellen McCarty	Daughter	5	Scholar	Swansea
	+ 2 children	-	1 & 3	-	Swansea
14	Edward Furlong	Head	40	Furnaceman, Copperworks	Ireland
	Mary Furlong	Wife	39	-	Ireland
	Nicholas Furlong	Son	12	Scholar	Ireland
	James Furlong	Son	10	Scholar	Ireland
	Margaret Furlong	Daughter	5	-	Swansea
	+ 3 children		-4 mths - 4 years	-	Swansea
16	Thomas Boland	Head	24	Labourer	Ireland
	Elizabeth Boland	Wife	22	-	Swansea
	+ 3 children	-	2 - 5	-	Swansea
18	Michael Coughlan	Head	28	Labourer	Ireland
	Bridgit Coughlan	Wife	25	-	Ireland
	Thomas Coughlan	Son	2	-	Swansea
	Martin Coughlan	Son	7 mths	-	Swansea
19	Richard Fitzgibbon	Head	60	Locksmith	Ireland
	Catharine Fitzgibbon	Wife	48	-	Ireland
	Catharine Fitzgibbon	Daughter	16	Scholar	Ireland
20	John Heeley	Head	25	Labourer	Ireland
	Ellen Heeley	Wife	26	-	Swansea
	John Heeley	Son	5	Scholar	Swansea
	+ 2 daughters		-5 mths & 3 years	-	Swansea
Mill Street					
1	Bridget Kealy	Head (W)	45	Gardener (Domestic Servant)	Ireland
	Bridget Kealy	Daughter	11	-	Ireland
	Mary Kealy	Daughter	14	General Servant	Ireland
	Bridget Glynn	Boarder	70	-	Ireland
2	Timothy Manery	Head	22	Labourer	Ireland
	Cathie Manery	Wife	22	-	London
	Mary Manery	Daughter	6 mths	-	Swansea
3	John Whelan	Head	39	Dock Labourer	Ireland
	Mary Whelan	Wife	37	-	Ireland
	Johannah Whelan	Daughter	13	Scholar	Ireland
	TimothyWhelan	Son	12	Scholar	Ireland
	Dennis Whelan	Son	10	Scholar	Ireland
	Patrick Whelan	Son	7	Scholar	Swansea
	John Whelan	Son	5	Scholar	Swansea
4	James Cocklan	Head	42	General Labour	Ireland
	Johannah Cocklan	Wife	40	-	Ireland
	Margaret Cocklan	Daughter	13	Scholar	Ireland

	David Khanhly	Boarder	25	Labourer	Ireland
	Mary Maharagh	Boarder	18	General Servant	Ireland
	Mary Shean	Boarder	16	-	Ireland
5	Joseph Murphy	Head	40	Labourer	Ireland
	Hanora Murphy	Wife	30	-	Ireland
	Julia Murphy	Daughter	10	Scholar	Swansea
	+ 4 children	-	1 - 7	-	Swansea
	Cornelius Leary	Head	60	Labourer	Ireland
	Mary Leary	Wife	43	-	Ireland
	Michael Leary	Son	23	Labourer	Ireland
	Timothy Leary	Son	20	Labourer	Ireland
6	Denis Crowly	Head	74	Labourer	Ireland
	Denis Crowly	Son	20	Labourer	Ireland
	Julia Murphy	G. child	10	-	Swansea
7	Patrick Begley	Head	38	Labourer	Ireland
	Julia Begley	Wife	34	-	Ireland
	Timothy Begley	Son	11	-	Neath
	John Begley	Son	6	-	Neath
	Jane Begley	Daughter	4	-	Swansea
	Catharine Begley	Daughter	1	-	Swansea
	Mary Condon	Lodger	24	General Servant	Ireland
	James Condon	Lodger	1	-	Swansea
8	James Barry	Head	26	Labourer	Ireland
	Mary Barry	Wife	26	-	Swansea
	John Barry	Son	4	-	Swansea
	Catharine Barry	Daughter	2	-	Swansea
	John Murphy	Boarder	20	Labourer	Ireland
9	Michael Foley	Head	34	Labourer	Ireland
	Ellen Foley	Wife	30	-	Ireland
	Thomas Foley	Son	13	Labourer in Fuel Works	Newport
	Johannah Foley	Daughter	5	-	Swansea
	+ 2 children		-2 mths & 2 years	-	Swansea
11	John Cannicombe	Head	35	General Labourer	Ireland
	Johannah Cannicombe	Wife	35	-	Ireland
	Mary Ann Cannicombe	Daughter	1	-	Swansea
	Bridget Smith	Lodger	40	Toy Seller	Ireland
15	John Nash	Head	36	Labourer	Ireland
	Ellen Nash	Wife	36	-	Ireland
	John Nash	Son	15	Labourer	Ireland
	Hanora Nash	Daughter	12	-	Swansea
	+ 2 children	-	2 & 8	-	Swansea

	John Mahony	Nephew	19	Labourer	Ireland
16	John Conoley	Head	50	General Labourer	Ireland
	Bridget Conoley	Wife	40	-	Ireland
	Mary Conoley	Daughter	19	Servant	Ireland
	Elizabeth Conoley	Daughter	15	Scholar	Ireland
	Margaret Conoley	Daughter	4	-	Swansea
	Jeremiah Atkins	Lodger	47	Stone Mason	Ireland
17	Ann Walsh	Head	37	Gardener (Domestic Servant)	Ireland
	Robert Walsh	Son	16	Mason Boy	Ireland
	James Mograage	Head	25	Labourer	Ireland
	Johannah Mograage	Wife	24	-	Ireland
	Patrick Baley	Head	40	Labourer	Ireland
	Ellen Baley	Wife	36	-	Ireland
	John Baley	Son	2	-	Swansea
19	John Slater	Head	35	Labourer	Ireland
	Sarah Slater	Wife	40	-	Haverfordwest
	Elizabeth Slater	Daughter	10	Scholar	Swansea
	Catherine Slater	Daughter	5	Scholar	Swansea
Mill Row					
5	William Carrol	Head	48	Labourer	Ireland
	Anne Carrol	Wife	52	-	Ireland
	Catherine Carrol	Daughter	16	Gardener (Domestic Servant)	Ireland
	Michael Carrol	Son	22	Sailor	Ireland
	William Carrol	Son	12	Mason Boy	Ireland
Bridge Street					
3	Elizabeth Ivory	Head	52	Lodging House Keeper	Ireland
	John Ivory	Son	12	Mason Boy	Swansea
	Richard Ivory	Son	7	-	Swansea
	Jeremiah Deasly	Boarder	60	Labourer	Ireland
	John Valentine	Boarder	61	Schoolmaster	Middlesex
5	Edmund Cotter	Head	53	Shoemaker & Lodging House Keeper	Ireland
	Mary Cotter	Wife	50	Shoe Binder	Ireland
	Elizabeth Cotter	Daughter	13	Milliner	Ireland
	+ 2 sons	-	6 & 8	Scholars	Ireland
10	John Callin	Head	30	General Dealer	Ireland
	Catharine Callin	Wife	30	-	Ireland
	Johanna Callin	Daughter	4	-	Swansea
	Edward Shearlock	Boarder	25	Labourer	Ireland
	Juley Dollenty	-	16	House Servant	Ireland

18	John White	Head	53	Labourer	Ireland
	Mary White	Wife	46	-	Ireland
	Jeremiah White	Son	24	Saddler	Ireland
	Mary Ann White	Daughter	17	-	Ireland
	Edward White	Son	15	Plumber Apprentice	Ireland
	Harriet White	Daughter	12	Scholar	Swansea
	Edward Kelly	Boarder	25	Labourer	Ireland
	Jeremiah Mahony	Head	24	Joiner	Ireland
	Ellen Mahony	Wife	20	Dressmaker	Ireland
20	Denis Conoley	Head	40	General Labourer	Ireland
	Catharine Conoley	Wife	46	-	Ireland
	Denis Conoley	Son	18	Labourer	London
	John Conoley	Son	12	Scholar	Bristol
	Thomas Doley	Stepson	28	Labourer	Ireland
	Mary Doley	Daughter	20	-	London
	Thomas Doley	Son	2	-	Swansea
	Jeremiah Driscoll	Stepson	24	Baker	London
	Juley Dollenty	Servant	16	-	Ireland
21	Jeremiah Ryan	Head	30	Labourer	Ireland
	Margaret Ryan	Wife	25	Dressmaker	Ireland
	Daniel Ryan	Son	9 mths	-	Swansea
23	Richard Rowland	Head	69	Glazier	Ireland
	Mary Rowland	Wife	60	-	Ireland
25	Edmund O'Keefe	Head	29	Labourer	Ireland
	Margaret O'Keefe	Wife	27	Dressmaker	Ireland
	Thomas O'Keefe	Son	1	-	Ireland
	Cornelius Sullivan	Boarder	50	Labourer	Ireland
	Thomas O'Keefe	Brother	31	Seaman Royal Marines	Ireland
26	Edward Casey	Head	52	Labourer	Ireland
	Margaret Casey	Wife	49	-	Swansea
	+ 3 children	-	9 - 21	-	Swansea
	William Reddaw	Head	26	Labourer	Ireland
	Mathew Reddaw	Brother	22	Labourer	Ireland
Well Street					
2	William Quirk	Head	40	Tailor	Ireland
	Mary Quirk	Wife	30	-	Ireland
	William Quirk	Son	17	Tailor	Ireland
	+ 6 children	-	3 - 16	-	Ireland
	Thomas Quirk	Son	1	-	Swansea
4	Timothy Brosnan	Head	26	Shoemaker	Ireland
	Margaret Brosnan	-	23	-	Ireland
	Mary Brosnan	Daughter	3	-	Swansea

	Margaret Brosnan	Daughter	1	-	Swansea
	John Brosnan	Head	23	Shoemaker	Ireland
	Ellen Brosnan	Wife	19	-	Ireland
5	Henry Cochin	Head	58	Shoemaker	Ireland
	Johannah Cochin	Wife	60	-	Ireland
	Hanora Ford	Boarder	64	-	Ireland
	Thomas Murphy	Boarder	35	General Labourer	Ireland
	Patrick Hennessy	Boarder	24	General Labourer	Ireland
	Ellen Hennessy	Wife	22	-	Ireland
7	Cornelius Collins	Head	25	General Labourer	Ireland
	Mary Collins	Wife	24	-	Ireland
	Margaret Collins	Daughter	3	-	Ireland
	Patrick Collins	Son	6 mths	-	Ireland
8	Michael Murphy	Head	23	Quarry Man	Ireland
	Margaret Murphy	Wife	21	-	Swansea
	Thomas Murphy	Son	1	-	Swansea
9	Margaret Brett	Head	55	Housekeeper	Ireland
	Michael Brett	Son	20	Labourer	Pontypool
	+ 2 children	-	16 & 18	-	Pontypool
11	Mary Casey	Head	65	-	Ireland
	Mary Casey	Daughter	30	General Servant	Ireland
	Julia Welsh	Head	40	Rag and Bone Gatherer	Ireland
	Elizabeth Welsh	Daughter	13	-	Ireland
	Daniel Welsh	Son	12	-	Ireland
14	Bartholomew Leeny	Head	37	Labourer	Ireland
	Catherine Leeny	Wife	33	-	Ireland
	+ 2 children	-	14 & 16	-	Ireland
	John Leeney	Son	10	-	Swansea
	+ 3 children		-2 mths - 8 years	-	Swansea
	Mary Leeney	G.Mother	80	-	Ireland
16	Patrick McTighe	Head	50	Labourer	Ireland
	Bridget McTighe	Wife	45	-	Ireland
	+ 2 sons	-	14 & 16	-	Ireland
	Bridget McTighe	Daughter	10	-	Swansea
	+ 3 children		-4 - 8 (2 twins)	-	Swansea
18	Bartholomew Hurley	Head	40	Shipper of Fuel	Ireland
	Catharine Hurley	Wife	41	-	Ireland
	Bartholomew Hurley	Son	1	-	Ireland
	James Lynch	Head	80	Labourer	Ireland
	John Barnett	S-in-law	26	Labourer	Ireland
	Hanora Barnett	Daughter	26	Housekeeper	Ireland

	Name	Relation	Age	Occupation	Birthplace
	Timothy Barnett	Nephew	8	-	Swansea
	Thomas Jenkins	Boarder	26	Labourer	Ireland
	Catharine Sullivan	Boarder	50	-	Ireland
	Mary Allon	Boarder	50	-	Ireland
Llangyfelach Street					
2	Pub:"Cork and Waterford Arms"				
	Edward Deady	Head	49	Victualler (Chelsea Pensioner)	Ireland
	Elizabeth Deady	Wife	41	-	Brecon
	Catharine Glinn	Servant	19	House Servant	Ireland
Well Street (Cont . . .)					
13	Patrick Sullivan	Head	42	Carter	Ireland
	Mary Sullivan	Wife	40	-	Ireland
	Patrick Sullivan	Son	3	-	Swansea
	Ellen Sullivan	Daughter	2	-	Swansea
Old Angel					
1	Timothy Fitzgerald	Head	77	Tin Man	Ireland
	George Jones	Boarder	33	Copperman	Ireland
	Martha Turner	Servant	22	House Servant	Swansea
	Moses Turner	Visitor	4	-	Swansea
2	Jeremiah Callahan	Head	44	Labourer	Ireland
	Bridget Callahan	Wife	35	-	Ireland
Angel Court					
1	Patrick Harrington	Head	30	Copper Ore Miner	Ireland
	Anne Harrington	Wife	28	-	Ireland
	Daniel Harrington	Son	8	-	Ireland
	Batt Harrington	Son	6	-	Ireland
	Patrick Harrington	Son	4	-	Ireland
	Edmund McCarey	Head	25	Labourer, Copperworks	Ireland
	Mary McCarey	Wife	24	-	Ireland
	Hanora McCarey	Daughter	2	-	Swansea
	Catharine Downey	M-in-law	50	-	Ireland
2	John O'Neal	Head	30	Labourer (Private in Coast Guard)	Ireland
	Ellen O'Neal	Wife	34	-	Ireland
	Hannah O'Neal	Daughter	3	-	Swansea
	Ellen O'Neal	Daugter	2	-	Swansea
3	John Borren	Head	36	Labourer	Ireland
	Mary Borren	Wife	39	-	Ireland
	John Borren	Son	14	-	Glostershire
	+ 3 sons	-	7 - 12	-	Glostershire

	Johannah Borren	Daughter	6	-	Swansea
	+ 2 daughters & 1 son		- 4 mths - 4 years	-	Swansea
4	Daniel Cassey	Head	50	Labourer	Ireland
	Abbey Cassey	wife	28	-	Ireland
	John Sullivan	Head	30	General Labourer	Ireland
	Julia Sullivan	Wife	30	-	Ireland
	Patrick Sullivan	Son	2	-	Dowlais
	Timothy Sullivan	Son	14 mths	-	Swansea
5	John Hennessy	Head	40	General Labourer	Ireland
	Julia Hennessy	Wife	30	-	Ireland
	Cathrine Hennessy	Daughter	13	-	London
	Anne Hennessy	Daughter	11	-	Newport
	John Hennessy	Son	6	-	Swansea
	+ 2 children	-	2 & 4	-	Swansea
	Patrick Donovan	Boarder	27	Working in Copperworks	Ireland
6	Patrick Regan	Head	50	Labourer	Ireland
	Johannah Regan	Wife	48	Housekeeper	Ireland
	Johannah Regan	Daughter	19	Scholar	Ireland
	Joseph Atkins	Boarder	32	Mason	Ireland
	+ 4 Welsh and 2 English Boarders				

Charles Street

1	'Masons Arms'				
	James Harries	Head	30	Ship Carpenter/ Victualler	Swansea
	Cornelius Moynahan	Boarder	24	Former Seaman	Ireland
2	Peter Lamb	Head	34	Rag & Bone Gatherer	Ireland
	Eliza Lamb	Wife	44	-	Tredegar
	William Lamb	Son	18	Tin Man	Cardiff
	+ 3 children	-	2 - 8	-	Merthyr
3	Timothy Cain	Head	54	Labourer	Ireland
	Ellen Cain	Wife	52	-	Ireland
	Michael Cain	Son	19	Labourer	Ireland
	+ 3 children	-	9 - 16	-	Ireland
4	Daniel Collins	Head	45	General Labourer	Ireland
	Hanora Collins	Wife	40	-	Ireland
	Julia Collins	Daughter	16	General Servant	Ireland
	Catharine Collins	Daughter	5	-	Swansea
	Daniel Collins	Son	2	-	Swansea
	William McCarthy	Boarder	39	General Labourer	Ireland
	John Thomas	Boarder	40	General Labourer	Ireland

5	John Sullivan	Head	40	Rag and Bone Gatherer	Ireland
	Hanora Sullivan	Wife	40	-	Ireland
	+ 3 children	-	2 - 10	-	Ireland
	Mary Warner	Boarder	40	Rag and Bone Gatherer	Ireland
	Sarah Warner	Daughter	6	-	Swansea
	John Warner	Son	3	-	Swansea
	Bridget Sullivan	-	30	General Servant	Ireland
	William Santry	Head	70	Rag and Bone Gatherer	Ireland
	Margaret Santry	Daughter	21	General Servant	Cardiff
	Elizabeth Santry	Wife	58	-	Ireland
6	Lary Bremner	Head	40	Labourer	Ireland
	Patrick Bremner	Son	19	Labourer	Swansea
	Ellen Bremner	Daughter	12	-	Swansea
	Catharine Leary	Head (W)	46	Toy Seller, etc	Ireland
	Cornelius Leary	Son	19	Labourer	Swansea
	Dennis Leary	Son	15	Mason Boy	Swansea
7	Michael Reardon	Head	40	Labourer	Ireland
	Mary Reardon	Wife	40	-	Ireland
	Johannah Reardon	Daughter	20	-	Ireland
	Michael Reardon	Son	5	-	Swansea
	Richard Bradey	Head	36	Labourer	Ireland
	Johannah Bradey	Wife	30	-	Ireland
	John Bradey	Son	4	-	Swansea
	Mary A Bradey	Daughter	14	-	Swansea
	Michael Conners	Head	25	Labourer	Ireland
	Johannah Conners	Wife	23	-	Ireland
	Mary Conners	Daughter	8	-	Swansea
8	John O'Brien	Head	32	Rag and Bone Gatherer	Ireland
	Catharine O'Brien	Wife	50	-	Ireland
	Morris Murphy	Head	37	Labourer	Ireland
	Margaret Murphy	Wife	34	-	Ireland
	Timothy Murphy	Son	4	-	Ireland
	John Murphy	Son	1	-	Swansea
	Michael Harrington	Head	42	Rag and Bone Gatherer	Ireland
	Margaret Harrington	Wife	34	-	Ireland
	Margaret Harrington	Daughter	8	-	Swansea
	+ 2 daughters	-	3 & 6	-	Swansea

	Michael Donovan	Boarder	30	General Labourer	Ireland
10	John Murphy	Head	40	-	Ireland
	Margaret Murphy	Wife	44	-	Ireland
	Julia Wilson	Boarder	46	-	Ireland
	+ 2 Welsh and 1 English Boarders				
11	Sarah Butler	Head	30	General Servant	Ireland
	Anne Leany	Boarder	24	General Servant	Swansea
	Mary Brien	Niece	2	-	Swansea
	Patrick Hackett	-	2½	-	Swansea
	Timothy Dacsey	Head	22	Labourer	Ireland
	Hanora Dacsey	Wife	21	-	Ireland
12	William Evans	Head	40	Labourer	Ireland
	Anne Evans	Wife	45	-	Ireland
	Jane Evans	Daughter	14	-	Swansea
	Catherine Welsh	Boarder	30	-	Ireland
	Timothy Welsh	Son	6	-	Swansea
	+ 2 daughters	-	2 & 4	-	Swansea
	Mike Sullivan	Head	25	General Servant	Ireland
	Margaret Sullivan	Wife	25	-	Ireland
	Patrick Sullivan	Son	3	-	Swansea
	Michael Sullivan	Son	1	-	Swansea
13	Richard Tobin	Head	35	General Labourer	Ireland
	Margaret Tobin	Wife	40	-	Ireland
	James Tobin	Son	13	-	Ireland
	Mary Tobin	Daughter	10	-	Ireland
	Michael Tobin	Son	9	-	Swansea
	+ 3 children		8 months - 7 years	-	Swansea
	Thomas Maroney	Boarder	14	Labourer	Swansea
14	John Sullivan	Head	50	-	Ireland
	Julia Sullivan	Wife	45	-	Ireland
	Bridget Sullivan	Daughter	16	Washerwoman	Ireland
	Hanorah Sullivan	Daughter	6	-	Swansea
	John Sullivan	Son	3	-	Swansea
	Ellen Sullivan	Daughter	2	-	Swansea
	Denis Donnovan	Head	44	General Labourer	Ireland
	Hannah Donnovan	Wife	32	-	Ireland
	Bridgit Donnovan	Daughter	12	-	Morriston
16	John Abbott	Head	23	Tailor	Ireland
	Julia Abbott	Wife	23	-	Ireland
	Mary Abbott	Daughter	2	-	Swansea
	John Abbott	Son	1	-	Swansea
	Hannorah Sullivan	Boarder	30	General Servant	Ireland

	John Sullivan	Son	5	Scholar	Swansea
	Johanah Harrington	Boarder	25	General Servant	Ireland
	Mary Harrington	Daughter	1	-	Swansea
	Martin Sullivan	Boarder	20	Tailor	Ireland
	Patrick Crowley	Boarder	20	General Labourer	Ireland
	William Lowney	Boarder	30	General Labourer	Ireland
	John Lowney	Boarder	25	General Labourer	Ireland
17	Timothy Murphy	Head	58	General Labourer	Ireland
	Catharine Murphy	Wife	38	-	Ireland
	John Murphy	Son	14	Mason Boy	Ireland
	Daniel Harrington	Boarder	30	General Labourer	Ireland
	Julia Harrington	Wife	22	-	Ireland
19	Alan Sullivan	Head	40	General Labourer	Ireland
	Mary Sullivan	Wife	32	-	Ireland
	Michael Sullivan	Son	15	Labourer in Chemical Works	Ireland
	+ 2 children	-	10 - 16	-	Ireland
	James Kailey	Head	23	General Labourer	Ireland
	Mary Kailey	Wife	24	-	Ireland
	Patrick Kailey	Son	3	-	Ireland
20	John Lynch	Head	40	Labourer, Copperworks	Ireland
	Ellen Lynch	Wife	40	-	Ireland
	John G Lynch	Son	12	Scholar	Swansea
	Jeremiah Lynch	Son	10 mths	-	Swansea
	Michael Shear	Head	30	Tailor	Ireland
	Mary Shear	Wife	32	-	Ireland
	Ellen Shear	Daughter	7	Scholar	Merthyr
	+ 2 sons	-	10 mths & 5 years	-	Swansea
21	Mary Sullivan	Head	32	-	Ireland
	Catharine Sullivan	Daughter	7	-	Swansea
	Margaret Sullivan	Daugter	5	-	Swansea
	Daniel Sullivan	Head	36	Tailor	Ireland
	Abbey Sullivan	Wife	34	-	Ireland
	Mary Sullivan	Daughter	11	Scholar	Swansea
	+ 4 sons	-	2 - 9	-	Swansea
	John Shehan	Boarder	20	Labourer	Ireland
	Job Healey	Boarder	18	Labourer	Ireland
	Abbey Sullivan	Boarder	50	-	Ireland
	Cornelius Sullivan	Boarder	20	General Labourer	Ireland
22	Catharine Sullivan	Head	30	Toy Seller	Ireland
	John Sullivan	Son	10	-	Ireland

	Catharine Sullivan	Daughter	6	-	Ireland
	Johanah Cournan	Sister	23	Toy Seller	Ireland
	Joan Cournan	Niece	1	-	Swansea
	Mary Sullivan	Boarder	26	General Servant	Ireland
	Mary White	Boarder	30	General Servant	Ireland
	John White	Son	5	-	Swansea
	Patrick Sullivan	Son	17	Rag and Bone Gatherer	Ireland
	Dan Sullivan	Son	27	General Labourer	Ireland
23	Cornelius Harrington	Head	48	Rag and Bone Gatherer	Ireland
	Mary Harrington	Wife	48	-	Ireland
	Daniel Harrington	Son	6	-	Swansea
	Tomothy Harrington	Son	3	-	Swansea
	Michael Heeley	Stepson	14	Carter	Ireland
	Nancy Demsey	Boarder	34	Rag and Bone Gatherer	Ireland
	Patrick Sullivan	Boarder	3	-	Swansea
	Nicholas Fitzgerald	Head	30	General Labourer	Ireland
	Mary Fitzgerald	Wife	30	-	Ireland
24	Michael Shanahar	Head	30	Labourer	Ireland
	Mary Shanahar	Wife	35	-	Ireland
	Mary Shanahar	Daughter	9	-	Liverpool
	Margaret Shanahar	Daughter	6	-	Liverpool
	Timothy Shaustian	Head	25	Labourer	Ireland
	Hanora Shaustian	Daughter	2	-	Swansea
25	Patrick Driscoll	Head	39	Labourer	Ireland
	Hanora Driscoll	Wife	38	-	Ireland
	James Driscoll	Son	9	-	Swansea
	+ 4 children		-6 mths - 8 years	-	Swansea
	John Buttermur	F-in-law	82	Former Labourer	Ireland
	Tomothy Hollernin	Head	21	Labourer	Swansea
	Margaret Hollernin	Wife	22	-	Swansea
26	James Sullivan	Head	36	General Labourer	Ireland
	Bridget Sullivan	Wife	40	-	Ireland
	Ellen Sullivan	Daughter	7	-	Swansea
	+ 3 children		-3 mths - 5 years	-	Swansea
	Mary Driscoll	M-in-Law	76	-	Ireland
	John Murphy	Head	30	General Labourer	Ireland
	Bridgett Murphy	Wife	28	-	Ireland
	Mary Murphy	Daughter	1	-	Swansea
27	Mary Williams	-	-	Grocery Shop	Sketty

28	Thomas Fitzgerald	Head	46	General Labourer	Ireland
	Ellen Fitzgerald	Wife	44	-	Ireland
	Patrick Fitzgerald	Son	10	Scholar	Ireland
	+ 2 children (daughters)	-	6 & 8	-	Ireland
	Daniel Dacy	Head	70	Labourer	Ireland
	Johanah Dacy	Wife	55	-	Ireland
	Daniel Dacy	Son	22	Labourer	Ireland
29	Denis Driscoll	Head	41	Labourer, Copperworks	Ireland
	Bridget Driscoll	Wife	39	-	Ireland
	Jane Driscoll	Daughter	12	-	Ireland
	+ 4 children	-	4 - 10	-	Ireland
	Catharine Driscoll	Mother	61	-	Ireland
30	'Ivy Bush'				
	Lewis Griffiths	-	-	Mason & Victular	Swansea
31	John McCarey	Head	58	Gardener/Servant	Ireland
	Catharine McCarey	Wife	34	-	Ireland
	John McCarey	Son	11	Scholar	Ireland
	Margaret McCarey	Daughter	13	Scholar	Ireland
	Daniel Murphy	Boarder	75	Former Labourer	Ireland
	Johannah Cockling	Boarder	70	-	Ireland
	Thomas Bryan	Head	30	Shoemaker	Ireland
	Catharine Bryan	Wife	25	-	Ireland
32	Denis Mahony	Head	42	Labourer	Ireland
	Catharine Mahony	Wife	32	-	Ireland
	Hanora Mahony	Daughter	13	Scholar	Swansea
	+ 3 sons	-	2 - 11	-	Swansea
	John Donovan	Head	40	Labourer	Ireland
	Ellen Donovan	Wife	34	-	Ireland
	Ellen Donovan	Daughter	15	Servant	Ireland
	Hanora Donovan	Daughter	1 month	-	Swansea
33	John Kating	Head	45	Rag and Bone Gatherer	Ireland
	Julia Kating	Wife	40	-	Ireland
	Julia Kating	Daughter	11	-	Ireland
	Kate Cronin	Boarder	40	Knitting Stockings	Ireland
	Bartholomew Lean	Head	26	Dock Labourer	Ireland
	Catharine Lean	Wife	28	-	Ireland
	Johannah Lean	Daughter	4	-	Ireland
34	Lawrence Sheary	Head	45	General Labourer	Ireland
	Margaret Sheary	Wife	35	General Labourer	Ireland
	Patrick Harnett	Head	47	-	Ireland

	+ 2 daughters	-	10 & 19	-	Ireland
	William Harnett	Son	2	-	Swansea
	Ellen Harnett	Daugter	8	-	Liverpool
35	Patrick Sullivan	Head	50	Rag and Bone Gatherer	Ireland
	Ellen Sullivan	-	40	-	Ireland
	Margaret Sullivan	Daughter	10	Scholar	Ireland
	Michael Sullivan	Son	2	-	Swansea
	Michael Sullivan	Head	27	Labourer Chemical Works	Ireland
	Bridget Sullivan	Wife	24	-	Ireland
	Thomas Sullivan	Son	2	-	Swansea
	Margaret Sullivan	Daughter	4 mths	-	Swansea
Back of Well Street					
1	Michael Lynch	Head	25	Labourer	Ireland
	Margaret Lynch	Wife	24	-	Ireland
	Ellen Lynch	Daughter	7	-	Swansea
	+ 2 children	-	1 & 4	-	Swansea
2 and 3 Owens Families of Swansea					
High Street					
172	Patrick Tracy	Head	26	Tailor	Ireland
	Hanora Tracy	Wife	24	-	Ireland
179	'The Thistle and Shamrock Inn'				
	Michael O'Brien	Head	39	Victular	Ireland
	Mary O'Brien Wife	34	-	-	Ireland
	Michael O'Brien Son	6	-	-	North Wales
	Mary O'Brien Daugter	4	-	-	Swansea
	Richard O'Brien	Son	1	-	Swansea
Back of					
179	Gerard Buckly	Head	36	Railway Labourer	Ireland
	Mary Buckly	Wife	42	-	Ireland
Mariner Street					
36	John Hilley	Head	56	Hawker	Ireland
	Margaret Hilley	Wife	39	-	Ireland
	Ellin McDonagh	Relation	8	Scholar	Ireland
	Michael Little	Lodger	60	Hawker	Ireland
	James White	Lodger	56	Hawker	Ireland
	Michael Heer	Lodger	46	Hawker	Ireland
	Mary Heer	-	45	Dressmaker	Ireland
	Catharine Burns	-	-	Hawker	Ireland
	Timothy McDonagh	-	20	Sailor	Ireland

	Name	Relation	Age	Occupation	Birthplace
Back Street					
42	Mathew Glaveen	Head	46	Labourer	Ireland
	Mary Glaveen	Wife	50	-	Ireland
	Julia Glaveen	-	15	Domestic Servant	Bristol
Lloyd Court					
4	James Morrissy	Head	28	Mason	Kilkenny
	Ellen Morrissy	Wife	32	-	Bandon, Co, Cork
	James Morrissy	Son	7	Scholar	Swansea
	+ 3 children	-	1 - 6	-	Swansea (1 at Merthyr)
	John Hearlelio	Lodger	34	Shoemaker	Ireland
	Anne Hearlelio	Lodger	25	Shoemaker's Wife	Ireland
	Margaret Hearlelio	Daughter	17 mths	-	Swansea
Queen Street					
16	Miles Sweeney	Head	60	Marine Store Dealer	Cork
	Catharine Sweeney	Wife	54	-	Cork
	Catharine Sweeney	Daughter	30	Washerwoman	Cork
	Bridget Sweeney	Daughter	27	Servant	Cork
	Edward Sweeney	Son	18	Labourer	Swansea
14	Thomas Driscole	Head	58	Plasterer	Cork
	Margaret Driscole	Wife	54	-	Cork
	Ellen Driscole	Daughter	22	Dressmaker	Cork
	William Driscole	Son	19	Ship Carpenter	Cork
Owen Court					
1	John Lundy	Son	40	Traveller	Ireland
	Anne Lundy	Mother(W)	63	-	Ireland
2	Patrick McCarthy	Head	42	Labourer	Cork
Tontine Street					
1	Denis Lane	Head(W)	80	Shoemaker	Ireland
	Anne Lane	Daughter	22	-	Risca, Mons.
	Honora Cockelne	-	67	Charwoman	Ireland
	Honora Cockelne	Daughter	17	Charwoman	Swansea
7	Bridget Green	Head	23	Charwoman	Ireland
	Johanna Galway	-	80	Lace Maker	Macroom, Co. Cork
	Mary Hagerty	Daughter	55	Lace Maker	Macroom, Co. Cork
11	John Fitzgerald	-	30	Boot & Shoe Maker	Wexford
	Mary Fitzgerald	Wife	30	Book Binder	Wexford

12	James McCormack	Head	65	Mason	Dublin
	Mary McCormack	Wife	65	-	Cork
	John Melvin	Lodger	40	Traveller	Mayo
14	Mary Curry	-	40	Traveller	Belfast
	John Curry	Son	7	Traveller	Belfast
39	Michael Lyons	Head	34	Labourer	Castle Town
	May Lyons	Wife	28	-	St Clears
	John Lyons	Son	6	-	St Clears
40	James Kilby	-	54	Excavator	Dublin
Swan Street					
3	John Healy	Head	41	Hawker	Ireland
	Sarah Healy	Wife	42	-	Bristol
	Maurice Daly	Head	30	Shoemaker	Cork
	Eliza Daly	Wife	34	-	Bristol
25	Mary O'Brien	Lodger (Widow)	52	Charwoman	Youghal, Co. Cork
Emma Street					
3	James Haley	Head	85	Labourer	Ireland
	Mary Haley	Wife	62	-	Ireland
	Daniel Haley	Son	22	Labourer	Landore
10	Patrick Dewett	Head	45	Labourer	Ireland
	Bridget Dewett	Wife	40	-	Bandon, Co. Cork
	William Dewett	Son	16	Labourer	St Giles, London
	Patrick Dewett	Son	13	Labourer	Swansea
	Michael Dewett	Son	6	-	Swansea
Grove Street					
1	Cornelius Green	Head	52	Labourer	Thornhill, Ireland
	Abby Green	Wife	49	-	Bear Island, Ireland
	Morris Green	Son	6	-	Castle Town, Ireland
	John Coughlin	Visitor	45	Traveller	Kirkhaven, Ireland
	Mary Ann Coughlin	Wife	34	-	Neath
	Ellen Coughlin	Daughter	2	-	Aberavon
	John Hurley	-	30	Labourer	Ireland (Deaf)
	Mary Hurley	Wife	34	-	Cork
	Mary Hurley	Daughter	9	-	Swansea
	Honora Hurley	Daughter	2	-	Swansea

	Mary Sullivan	Visitor	19	Servant	Waterford
	Denis Sullivan	Lodger	22	Labourer	Thornhill, Ireland
2	Thomas Leary	Head	52	General Dealer	Ireland
	Julia Leary	Wife	54	-	Ireland
	May Leary	-	16	-	Ireland
3	Dennis Sullivan	Head	32	Copperman	Ireland
	Catharine Sullivan	Wife	26	-	Ireland
	Mary Sullivan	Daughter	3	-	Swansea
	Catherine Sullivan	Daughter	1	-	Swansea
	James Armstrong	Head	23	Labourer	Ireland
	Julia Armstrong	Wife	22	-	Ireland
	Jane Armstrong	Daughter	13	-	Swansea
	John Murphy	Lodger	21	Copperman	Ireland
4	Patrick Tray	Head	37	Labourer	Waterford
	Mary Tray	Wife	44	-	Cork
	Mary Sullivan	Daughter	16	-	Cork
	Patrick Tray	Son	5	-	Swansea
	William Murray	Head	28	Labourer	Cork
	Bridgit Murray	Wife	26	-	Cork
	Bridgit Murray	Daughter	4	-	Cork
	May Murray	Daughter	14 mths	-	Swansea
5	John Coughlin	Head	80	Tailor	Cork
	Margaret Coughlin	Wife	70	-	Cork
	Patrick Murray	Head	40	Shoemaker	Cork
	Catherine Murray	Wife	40	-	Cork
	Cornelius Murray	Son	14	-	Cork
	Mary Ann Murray	Daughter	9	Cork	
6	Michael Murray	Head	45	Labourer	Cork
	Ellen Murray	Wife	40	-	Cork
	Daniel McCarthy	Boarder	22	Labourer	Cork
Llangyfelach Street					
14	Mathew Green	Head	36	-	Cork
	Julia Green	Wife	27	-	Cork
	John Green	Son	10	Scholar	Cork
	Patrick Green	Son	5	Scholar	Swansea
	+ 2 children		-2 mths & 4 years	-	Ireland
	Ellen Walsh	Lodger	49	-	Castle Martin
35	James Higgings	Head	40	Haulier	Ireland
	Catharine Higgings	Wife	38	-	Ireland
	Charles Higgings	Son	9	-	Swansea
	+ 2 children		-7 years & 4 years	-	Swansea

	Hanora Paterson	Lodger	60	-	Ireland
36	Thomas Flynn	Head	32	Labourer	Cork
	Mary Flynn	Wife	30	-	Cork
	Elizabeth Flynn	Daughter	9	-	Swansea
	Marian Flynn	Daughter	2	-	Swansea
37	Edward Barry	Head	60	Carpenter	Ireland (n.k.)
	Elizabeth Barry	Wife	58	-	Ireland
	David Barry	Son	20	-	Ireland
	Elizabeth Barry	Daughter	18	-	Ireland
	John Shea	S-in-law	21	Haulier	Ireland
38	Patrick Flynn	Head	50	Labourer	Cork
	John Flynn	Son	24	Labourer	Cork
	Timothy Flynn	Son	29	Labourer	Cork
	+ 4 children	-	17 - 26	-	Cork
	John Bury	S-in-law	22	-	Cork
	John Sullivan	S-in-law	26	-	Cork
39	Michael Callaghan	Head	28	Haulier	Cork
	Hanora Callaghan	Wife	40	-	Cork
	John Callaghan	Son	17	Labourer	Cork
	Catharine Callaghan	Daughter	15	-	Cork
	Michael Callaghan	Son	8	Swansea	
	James Callaghan	Son	1	-	Swansea
43	Michael O'Connell	Head	51	Labourer	Ireland (n.k.)
	Hanora O'Connell	Wife	48	-	Ireland
	James O'Connell	Son	15	-	Ireland
	John O'Connell	Son	13	-	Ireland
	Stephen O'Connell	Son	10	Scholar	Ireland
	Anastasia O'Connell	-	20	Dressmaker	Ireland
	Abby O'Connell	Daughter	2	-	Swansea
	Jeremiah Connelly	S-in-law	23	Labourer	Ireland
	Mary Connelly	G.child	1 mth	-	Swansea
44	John Murphy	Head	59	Labourer	Cork
	Anora Murphy	Wife	50	-	Cork
	William Murphy	Son	21	Mariner	Swansea
	+ 4 children	-	2 - 11	8 + 11 Labouring	Swansea
	Marine Cinney	Lodger	38	-	Cork
	Denis Cinney	Lodger	18	Labourer	Swansea
47	Jeremiah Sullivan	Head	70	Labourer	Cork
	Mary Sullivan	Wife	50	-	Cork
	Hanora Sullivan	Daughter	24	-	Swansea
	John Sullivan	Son	5	-	Carlow, Ireland

	John Doyle	S-in-law	35	Labourer	Swansea
	Mary Doyle	Wife	30	-	Swansea
	+ 2 daughters	-	7 & 14	-	Swansea
48	Patrick Marra	Head	50	Shoemaker	Dungarvan, Co. Waterford
	Mary Marra	Wife	40	-	Kilkenny
	Nicholas Walsh	Lodger	60	Shoemaker	Kilkenny
	Robert Deeble	Lodger	20	Labourer	Cork
49	Thomas Dally	Head	46	Labourer	Cork
	Margaret Dally	Wife	43	-	Cork
	John Dally	Son	16	Labourer	Swansea
	+ 2 children	-	9 & 11	Scholars	Swansea
	John Wollarn	S-in-law	14	Mason	Swansea
	Mary Wollarn	Daughter	-	Dressmaker	Swansea
	Lary Brinel	Lodger	40	Labourer	Kilkenny
	Patrick Brinel	Son	19	Labourer	Kilkenny
	Ellen Brinel	Daughter	12	-	Kilkenny
50	William Fitzgerald	Head	46	Labourer	Cork
	Mary Fitzgerald	Wife	42	-	Cork
	Johanna Fitzgerald	Daughter	20	Servant	Swansea
	+ 3 children	-	11 - 18	-	Swansea
	William Larking	Visitor	36	Labourer	Cork
	Ellen Griffiths	Visitor	24	Dressmaker	Kilkenny
51	Anthony Kelly	Head	35	Labourer	Co. Roscommon
	Catharine Kelly	Wife	25	-	Swansea
	+ 4 children	-	1 - 5	-	Swansea
	Ann Sullivan	S-in-law	12	-	Swansea
52	Michael Vaughan	Head	40	Labourer	Cork
	Ellen Vaughan	Wife	36	-	Cork
	Hannah Vaughan	Daughter	8	Scholar	Swansea
	+ 3 children	-	1 - 6	-	Swansea
	Caroline Corkoran	Visitor	30	Widow	Cork
	James Furlong	Son	3	-	Swansea
	Patrick Sullivan	Head	25	Labourer	Cork
	Mary Sullivan	Wife	23	-	Cork
	May Sullivan	Daughter	2	-	Swansea
53	Ann Connelly	Head (W)	60	House Keeper	Cork
	Jeremiah Connelly	Son	22	Labourer	Swansea
	Edward Connelly	Son	10	Scholar	Swansea
	Lary Flemin	Boarder	30	Labourer	Cork
	Johana Flemin	Wife	30	-	Cork

	Name	Relation	Age	Occupation	Birthplace
	Mary Flemin	Daughter	7	-	Swansea
	+ 2 children	-	2 - 11	-	Swansea
54	Dennis Kineary	Head	45	Tailor	Ireland (n.k.)
	Judy Kineary	Wife	46	-	Ireland
	+ 2 daughters	-	10 & 13	-	Ireland
	John Green	Lodger	35	Labourer	Cork
	Julia Green	Wife	30	-	Cork
55	William Taylor	Head	48	Labourer	Ireland (n.k.)
	Ellen Taylor	Wife	36	-	Dungarvon, Co. Waterford
	Thomas Taylor	Son	14	Labourer	Swansea
56	John Griskin	Head	36	Labourer	Cork
	Julia Griskin	Wife	40	-	Kerry
	James Griskin	Son	6	-	Swansea
	+ 2 daughters	-	2 & 4	-	Swansea
	Thomas Wilson, Wife and 2 children				Swansea
	Alexander Shean	Lodger	60	Labourer	Kerry
	Elizabeth Shean	Wife	35	-	Cork
	Mary Sullivan	-	34	Labourer's Widow	Cork
	Mary Sullivan	Daughter	15	Servant	Cork
	Bridget Sullivan	Daughter	11	Scholar	Swansea
	+ 2 other children	-	1 & 4	-	Swansea
57	Mary Connel	Head (W)	40	-	Waterford
	John Fitzgerald	Son	14	Labourer	Waterford
Ann Street					
1	Jeremiah O'Brien	Head	50	Labourer	Ireland (n.k.)
	Mary O'Brien	Wife	49	-	Ireland
	+ 2 sons & 1 daughter	-	16 - 20	- Ireland	
	John Callahan	Boarder	50	Labourer	Ireland
2	Thomas Hart	Head	43	Labourer	Cork
	Margaret Hart	Wife	43	-	Cork
	John Hart	Son	17	Labourer	Cork
	Mary Hart	Daughter	14	-	Cork
	Ellen Hart	Daughter	8	-	London
	Jeremiah Hart	Son	5	-	Swansea
	William Hart	Son	15 mths	-	Swansea
	John Nahaun	Head	39	Labourer	Cork
	Mary Nahaun	Wife	40	-	Cork
	Ellen Nahaun	Daughter	8	-	Swansea
	+ 3 children		- 1 mth - 5 years	-	Swansea
3	Daniel O'Brien	Head	45	Labourer	Ireland

	Ellen O'Brien	Wife	46	-	Ireland
	Anora O'Brien	Daughter	18	-	Swansea
	+ 5 children	-	1 - 15	-	Swansea
	John Sullivan	Boarder	50	Labourer	Ireland
	Jeremiah O'Brien	Boarder	18	Labourer	Ireland
	Ellen O'Brien	Widow	70	-	Ireland
	Julia O'Brien	Widow	92	-	Ireland
	Timothy McCarthy	Head	32	Labourer	Cork
	Mary McCarthy	Wife	31	-	Cork
	Timothy McCarthy	Son	12	-	Cork
	+ 3 daughters	-	1 - 9	-	Swansea
4	Patrick O'Brien	Head	25	Labouring, Copperworks	Waterford
	Catharine O'Brien	Wife	20	-	Waterford
	John Cocklin	Boarder	15	labourer	Waterford
	Mary Driscole	Visitor	40	Widow	Cork
	Ann Wilson	Head (W)	50	-	Cork
	George Wilson	Son	15	Labourer	Swansea
	Michael Megrouh	Head	45	Labourer	Waterford
	Bridget Megrouh	Wife	44	-	Waterford
	Bridget Megrouh	Daughter	17	-	Waterford
7	Jeremiah Shea	Head	30	General Labourer	Ireland
	Mary Shea	Wife	30	-	Ireland, Kerry
	Phoebe Shea	Sister	14	-	Ireland, Cork
	Mary Shea	Daughter	10	-	Ireland, Cork
	Jeremiah Shea	Son	7	-	Swansea
	+ 2 children	-	3 & 7	-	Swansea
8	Michael Connors	Head	39	Labourer	Ireland
	Ann Connors	Wife	40	-	Ireland
	Catharine Connors	Daughter	19	Married	Ireland
	Patrick Fitzgibbons	S-in-law	20	Labourer	Ireland
	+ 2 children	-	8 & 14	-	Ireland
	Mary Nonner	Boarder	22	Servant	Ireland
	Joseph Brenen	Boarder	40	Labourer	Ireland
	Julia Brenen	Wife	-	-	Ireland
	+ 2 children		-7 mths & 5 years	-	Swansea
9	Ugene Cunnigham	Head	35	Labourer	Cork
	Mary Cunnigham	Wife	20	-	Cork
	John Cunnigham	Son	8	-	Swansea
	+ 3 sons		-4 mths - 4 years	-	Swansea
	John McCarthy	Head	55	Labourer	Ireland
	Nancy McCarthy	Wife	30	Dressmaker	Ireland, Cork

	Robert Welsh	Head	25	Labourer	Ireland, Cork
	Margaret Welsh	Wife	32	-	Ireland, Kerry
	Michael Welsh	Son	8	-	Ireland, Waterford
	Robert Welsh	Son	2	-	Waterford
10	Augustus Richfield	Head	38	Labourer	Waterford
	Mary Richfield	Wife	39	-	Waterford
	May & ? Richfield	Daughters	18 & 12	-	Waterford
	Thomas Richfield	Son	6	-	Swansea
	Ellen Richfield	Daughter	2	-	Swansea
	James Sullivan	Boarder	30	Labourer	Ireland
	Patsy Sullivan	Wife	25	-	Ireland
	+ 3 children	-	5,6 & 7	-	Ireland
	John Sullivan	Son	2	-	Swansea
11	Timothy Shean	Head	50	Labourer	Ireland
	Mary Shean	Wife	45	-	Ireland
	Edward Shean	Son	12	-	Swansea
	+ 3 children	-	3 - 10	-	Swansea
12	Ellen Shean	Head	44	-	Kerry
	Anora Shean	Daughter	17	-	Kerry
	Ellen Shean	Daughter	11	-	Cork
	John Shean	Son	8	-	Llanidloes
	Patrick Shean	Son	3	-	Swansea
	Mary Ann Shean	Daughter	1	-	Swansea
	Patrick Corcon	Lodger	24	Labourer	Kerry
	Margaret Corcon	Wife	19	-	Kerry
	John Corcon	Son	2	-	Swansea
13	Mathew Cavanah	Head	40	Labourer	Ireland
	Mary Cavanah	Wife	48	-	Ireland
	+ 2 children	-	10 & 18	-	Ireland
	Edward Corbett	Head	38	Labourer	Ireland
	Rebeca Corbett	Wife	30	-	Ireland
	Edward Corbett	Son	12	-	Swansea
	+ 3 other sons	-	2 - 10	-	Swansea
15	Timothy Shea	Head	63	Labourer	Cork
	Bridget Shea	Wife	46	-	Tipperary
	Margaret Flyn	Boarder	30	-	Waterford
	William Eaton	Lodger	23	Labourer	Ireland, (n.k.)
	Margaret Eaton	Wife	26	-	Waterford
	William Eaton	Son	4	-	Swansea
	Ellen Flynn	Lodger	35	-	Waterford
	Joseph Flynn	Son	10	-	Waterford
	+ 2 other children	-	-	-	Waterford

	Margaret Flynn	Daughter	11 mths	-	Swansea
16	James Murphy	Head	39	Labourer	Leamington, Warwickshire
	Catharine Murphy	Wife	35	-	Dublin
	2 children	-	10 & 6	-	Birmingham & Bath respectively
	Frank Murphy	Son	3	-	Swansea
	Andrew Murphy	Son	9 mths	-	Swansea
	Richard Lyons	Head	45	Labourer	Cork
	Mary Lyons	Wife	40	-	Cork
	Joseph Lyons	Son	11 mths	-	Swansea
17	Thomas Donnell	Head	35	Haulier	Tipperary
	Joannah Donnell	Wife	36	-	Kerry
	Margaret Donnell	Daughter	4	-	Swansea
	James Donnell	Son	1	-	Swansea
18	Michael Sheen	Head	50	Marine Store Dealer	Kilmore
	Mary Sheen	Wife	30	-	Kerry
	Jeremiah Sheen	Son	15	Labourer	Kerry
	Mary Sheen	Daughter	10	-	Kerry
	Catharine Sheen	Daughter	9	-	Swansea
	+ 4 children		-4 mths - 7 years	-	Swansea
19	William Barnes	Head	30	Labourer	Waterford
	Ellen Barnes	Wife	23	-	Waterford
	Mary Barnes	Daughter	7	-	Swansea
	+ 3 other children	-	1 - 5	-	Swansea
	Catharine McDonald	S-in-law	25	-	Waterford
	Morris Cummins	Head	25	Labourer	Waterford
	Ellen Cummins	Wife	26	-	Waterford
	Patrick Cummins	Son	6	-	Waterford
	Ellen Cummins	Daughter	7 mths	-	Swansea
20	Jeremiah O'Brien	Head	50	Hawker	Kerry
	Julia O'Brien	Wife	48	-	Kerry
21	Jeremiah McCarthy	Head	40	Labourer	Kilmore
	Joannah McCarthy	Wife	40	-	Kerry
	Annah McCarthy	Daughter	8	-	Cork
	Stephen McCarthy	Son	5	-	Cork
	James McCarthy	Son	5 mths	-	Swansea
	Ellen McCarthy	Boarder	100	-	Kerry
22	Dennis Hayes	Head	37	Labourer	Cork
	Mary Hayes	Wife	31	-	Cork
	Joseph Hayes	Son	8	-	Swansea

	+ 2 children		-1 mth & 5 years	-	Swansea
	Patrick Bryant	Boarder	55	Labourer	Tipperary
23	Michael Callaghan	Head	29	Labourer	Cork
	Ellen Callaghan	Wife	28	-	Cork
	Daniel Callaghan	Son	6	-	Swansea
	+ 2 sons	-	1 & 4	-	Swansea
	Catharine Callaghan	Widow	60	-	Cork
	John Barry	Boarder	27	Labourer	Cork
	Margaret Barry	Wife	27	-	Limerick
	Edmund Barry	Son	1	-	Swansea
24	James Welsh	Head	50	Labourer	Cork
	Mary Welsh	Wife	40	-	Cork
	Thomas Welsh	Son	20	Mariner	Swansea
	William Welsh	Son	15	Collier	Swansea
	+ 4 children	-	1 - 13	-	Swansea
	Thomas North	Head	60	Carpenter	Ireland
	Ellen North	Wife	50	-	Ireland
	Bridget North	Daughter	12	-	Swansea
25	Michael O'Neil	Head	39	Labourer	Ireland
	Margaret O'Neil	Wife	32	-	Ireland
	Francis O'Neil	Son	12	-	Ireland
	Margaret O'Neil	Daughter	6	-	Swansea
	Elloner O'Neil	Daughter	3	-	Swansea
	Cornelius Crawley	Head	25	Labourer	Ireland
	Mary Crawley	Wife	22	-	Ireland
	Ann Nora Crawley	Daughter	2	-	Swansea
	Catharine Crawley	Daughter	2	-	Swansea
	Dennis Murphy	Boarder	50	Labourer	Ireland
	Ellen Murphy	Daughter	19	-	Ireland
26	Thomas SampsonKitchen	Head	54	Boot Lace Maker	Whitechapel, London
	Francis Sampson	Wife	48	-	Kilarney
	Mary Ann	Daughter	11	-	Swansea
27	John Bryan	Head	55	Labourer	Waterford
	Mary Bryan	Wife	52	-	Waterford
	Thomas Welch	Head	30	Labourer	Kilmore
	Margaret Welch	Wife	28	-	Kilmore
	Patrick Welch	Son	6	-	Kilmore
	Catharine Welch	Daughter	18 mths	-	Swansea
28	Michael Hally	Head	36	Labourer	Waterford
	Mary Hally	Wife	36	-	Waterford
	+ 3 children	-	8 - 15	-	Waterford

	Name	Relation	Age	Occupation	Birthplace
	John Hally	Son	6	-	Swansea
	+ 2 children	-	1 - 4	-	Swansea
	Patrick Kennedy	Lodger	35	Labourer	Waterford
Little Grove Street					
1	John Kelly	Head	50	Hay Dealer	Kerry
	Mary Kelly	Wife	38	-	Kerry
	John Kelly	Son	11	Scholar	Swansea
	Thomas Kelly	Son	8	Scholar	Swansea
	Daniel Driscoll	Head	36	Labourer	Cork
	Mary Driscoll	Wife	25	-	Cork
	John Driscoll	Son	1	-	Swansea
2	Humphrey Driscoll	Head	64	Labourer	Ireland
	Caroline Driscoll	Wife	60	-	Ireland
	+ 3 children	-	12 - 18	-	Ireland
3	John Sullivan	Head	24	Marine Dealer	Cork
	Michael Sullivan	Brother	20	Marine Dealer	Cork
	Daniel Sullivan	Brother	15	Haulier	Cork
Pont Glas y Dwr					
1	Michael Kilfoye	Head	40	Labourer	Tipperary
	Ellen Kilfoye	Wife	35	-	Tipperary
	2 children	-	16 & 18	-	Tipperary
	Michael Kilfoye	Son	10	-	Swansea
	+ 2 sons	-	6 & 8	-	Swansea
2	Thomas Husband	Head	50	Musician	Ireland
	Mary Husband	Wife	49	-	Ireland
	Michael Husband	Son	19	Labourer	Ireland
	+ 2 daughters	-	14 & 16	-	Ireland
	Joannah Husband	Daughter	6	Blind from Birth	London
	Ellen Casey	M-in-law	53	Widow	Cork
	Daniel Casey	Son	24	Violin Player	Cork
	Ann Casey	Daughter	13	-	Liverpool
6	Catharine Foley	Head(W)	60	-	Ireland
	John Brien	S-in-law	38	-	Ireland
	Margater Brien	Wife	34	-	Ireland
	Mary Brien	Daughter	8	-	Swansea
	+ 3 children	-	1 - 5	-	Swansea
	Mary Sullivan	Lodger	60	Widow	Ireland
8	Daniel Sullivan	Head	45	Furnace Copperman	Cork
	Mary Sullivan	Wife	36	-	Cork
	+ 6 children	-	1 - 15	-	Swansea
	Ellen McCarthy	Head	42	-	Swansea
	Catherine McCarthy	Daughter	10	-	Swansea

	+ 4 children	-	1 - 9	-	Swansea
12	Edward Murphy	Head	56	Labourer	Ireland
	Ellen Murphy	Wife	52	-	Ireland
	+ 2 sons	-	13 & 20	Labourers	Swansea
	James Millan	Boarder	29	Labourer	Swansea
13	Edward Allworth	Head	30	Labourer	Ireland
	Mary Allworth	Wife	38	-	Ireland, Cork
	Edward Allworth	Son	9	Scholar	Swansea
	Mary Jane Allworth	Daughter	3	Scholar	Swansea
	James Allworth	Son	4	-	Swansea
	Margaret Morgan	S-in-law	40	Dressmaker	Ireland, Cork
	Ellen Murphy	Boarder	40	Widow	Kerry
	Ellen Murphy	Boarder	24	Dressmaker	Kerry
	Mary Sullivan	Boarder	25	Washerwoman	Cork
	Mary Sullivan	-	1	-	Swansea
14	Bartholomew O'Brien	Head	28	Marine Store Dealer	Kerry
	Anora O'Brien	Wife	27	-	Cork
	John O'Brien	Son	6	-	Swansea
	+ 2 sons	-	3 & 5	-	Swansea
	Florence O'Brien	Father	70	Labourer	Kerry
	Bridget O'Brien	Wife	60	-	Kerry
15	Florence Brine	Head	40	Labourer	Kerry
	Mary Brine	Wife	35	-	Kerry
	+ 3 sons & 1 daughter	-	5,15,1	-	Kerry
	William Brine	Boarder	17	Labourer	Cork
	Joannah Simon	Boarder	35	-	Cork
	Mary Sullivan	Boarder	2	-	Swansea
16	John Mahony	Head	40	Labourer	Ireland
	Julia Mahony	Wife	30	-	Ireland
	Michael Mahony	Son	6	-	Swansea
	+ 2 children		-1 mth & 3 years	-	Swansea
	Ellen Murphy	Boarder	26	Dressmaker	Ireland
	John Brosneen	Head	50	Labourer	Ireland
	Ann Brosneen	Wife	30	-	Ireland
	+ 2 children		-1 mth & 2 years	-	Swansea
18	John Sullivan	Head	26	Labourer	Ireland
	Margaret Sullivan	Wife	22	-	Ireland
	David Sullivan	Son	3	-	Swansea
	Henry Sullivan	Son	8 mths	-	Swansea
	Peter O'Brien	Head	32	Labourer	Ireland
	Catharine O'Brien	Wife	24	-	Ireland

	Margaret O'Brien	Daughter	9	-	Aberavon
	+ 2 children		-1 mth & 4 years	-	Swansea
19	Dennis Leary	Head	60	Labourer	Cork
	Ellen Leary	Wife	50	-	Cork
	Jeremiah Leary	Son	18	Labourer	Swansea
Little Emma Street					
2	John Sullivan	Head	46	Marine Store Dealer	Kenmere, Co. Kerry
	Catharine Sullivan	Wife	30	-	Waterford
	Mary Sullivan	Daughter	2	-	Swansea
	Julia Sullivan	Daughter	1	-	Swansea
	Mary Wheelan	M-in-law	80	-	Ireland
	John Foley	Head	40	Labourer	Ireland
	Mary Foley	Wife	38	-	Ireland
4	James Nugent	Head	32	Copperman	Dublin
	Hannah Nugent	Wife	34	-	Dublin
	James Nugent	Son	11	-	St David's
	+ 4 children	-	1 - 9	-	Swansea
5	James Quin	Head	40	Labourer	Brockney, Ireland
	Margaret Quin	Wife	36	-	Brockney, Ireland
	+ 5 children	-	13 - 20	-	Brockney, Ireland
	Michael Rogers	Boarder	34	Labourer	Ireland
	Bridget Rogers	Wife	36	-	Ireland
Brynmellin: No Irish					
Carmarthen Road					
3	Francis Ryan	Head	59	Labourer (Dock)	Ireland
	Alice Ryan	Wife	45	-	Ireland
48	Dennis Keefe	Head	28	Copperman	Ireland
	Hannah Keefe	Wife	28	-	Tenby
	+ 3 children		-3 mths - 3 years	-	Swansea
63	Daniel Kilman	Head	50	Copper Labourer	Ireland
	Ellen Kilman	Wife	40	-	Ireland
	+ 5 children	-	4 - 15	-	Swansea
	John Keefe	Lodger	26	Mason's Labourer	Ireland
	Catharine Keefe	Wife	24	-	Ireland
65	Henry Warner	Head	52	Colliery Labourer	Ireland
	Ellen Warner	Wife	42	-	Ireland
	+ 3 children	-	1 - 7	-	Swansea

Hannah Warner	-	14	General Servant	Swansea
Mary Keefe	Visitor	23	-	Ireland

Bibliography

Primary Sources

(a). Manuscripts

SWANSEA CITY ARCHIVES OFFICE

EA310. Estates Department, Miscellaneous Maps and Plans.

FAC86. Facsimile documents relating to St Joseph's Church.

HE1. Annual Reports of the Medical Officer of Health, 1874-.

MP/Est 1. Borough of Swansea, Estate Plan and Report, 1850.

MP/LBH/Swansea/1. Swansea Local Board of Health, Survey of the Borough of Swansea, 1852.

MP/LBH/Swansea/2. Swansea Local Board of Health, Survey of Swansea, showing Water Supplies, 1854.

MP/Tithe/Swansea. Copy of Tithe Map for Swansea Parish, 1843.

P/PR58. Photographic Collection, dossier for Greenhill & Dyfatty areas.

TC4/P & G. Borough of Swansea, Minutes of the Property (and General Purposes) Committee, 1844-.

TC67. Records of the Swansea Local Board of Health and Urban Sanitary Authority, 1850-.

TC70. Records of the Swansea Burial Board, 1855-.

TR/RB/S. Town and Franchise of Swansea, Poor Rate Books, 1845-.

UNIVERSITY COLLEGE OF SWANSEA LIBRARY

St David's Priory Records

1. St David's Church Register, 1808-39.
2. St David's Priory Register of Marriages, 1840-64.
3. St David's Priory Register of Baptisms,18 November 1839 - 31 July 1852.
4. St David's Priory Baptismal Index, 1805-1950.

Swansea Statistical Society of the Royal Institution of South Wales

1. Statistical 1; Survey of the Town and Franchise of Swansea by George Jones, 1837.

2. Statistical 2; Swansea Statistical Survey of October 1839.

Book of Orders, 1569 - 1682.

Common Hall Book and Book of Orders, 1547 - 1665.

Borough of Swansea

Swansea Corporation Rate Book of 1842

(b) Documents in Print

Newspapers: The *Cambrian*, 1840-1860.
The *Swansea Journal*, 1843.
Y Diwygiwr, xvii (1848).
The *South Wales Evening Post*, 12-16 September 1988.

Health and Other Reports:

DE LA BECHE, H.T., *(Health of Towns Commission) Report on the State of Bristol, Bath, Frome, Swansea, Merthyr Tydfil and Brecon* (London, 1845)

CLARK, G.T., *Report to the General Board of Health on a Preliminary Inquiry into the Sewage, Drainage and Supply of Water, and the Sanitary Condition of the Inhabitants of the Town and Borough of Swansea.* (London, 1849).

MICHAEL, W.H., *First Quarterly Report on the Sickness and Mortality of the Borough of Swansea from the First of October, 1853, to the First of January, 1854: Together with a Supplementary Report on the Cholera in Swansea in 1849* (Swansea, 1854).

MICHAEL, W.H., *The Medical Report on the Sickness and Mortality of the Borough of Swansea for the year 1854 together with maps and Appendix* (Swansea, 1856).

The National Library of Wales, Calendar of the Diary of Lewis Weston Dillwyn, vol. II, 18 November 1823 - 31 December 1833.

Reports of the Commissioners of Inquiry into the state of Education in Wales, Part 1 Carmarthen, Glamorgan and Pembroke (London,1847).

Religious Census of 1851

Census of 1841, 1851 and 1861.

Special Report on Surnames in Ireland, Appendix to Twenty-Ninth Report of the Registrar-General (Dublin, 1894).

Secondary Authorities

ALBAN, J.R., *St Joseph's Church and Greenhill. A Centenary Exhibition* (Swansea, 1988).

ALBAN, J.R., 'The Wider World', *The City of Swansea. Challenges and Change*, ed. R.A. Griffiths (Stroud, 1990), pp. 114-29.

ATTWATER, D., *The Catholic Church in Modern Wales. A Record of the Past Century* (London, 1935).

BAINBRIDGE, A., *Crime in Nineteenth-Century Wales: A Preliminary Report on the Sources and Character of Crime in Welsh Communities* (Swansea, 1975).

BEECH, C., 'The Social and Economic effects of the Irish Potato Famine' (Unpublished B.Sc. Home Economics dissertation, University College Cardiff, 1982).

BOSSE-GRIFFITHS, K., 'The Leper Stone of Llanrhidian', *Gower*, xix (1968), 72-75.

BOWEN, E.G., *The Settlements of the Celtic Saints in Wales* (Cardiff, 1956).

BOWEN, E.G., *Saints, Seaways and Settlements in the Celtic Lands* (Cardiff, 1977).

CARTER, H., 'The Vale of Glamorgan and Gower', *Wales. A Physical, Historical and Regional Geography*, ed. E.G. Bowen, (London, 1957), pp.401-30.

CARTER, H., 'The Structure of Glamorgan Towns in the Nineteenth Century', *Glamorgan County History, vi: Glamorgan Society, 1780-1980*, ed. Prys Morgan (Cardiff, 1988), pp.151-71.

CHARLES, B.G., *Old Norse Relations with Wales* (Cardiff, 1934).

CONNOLLY, G.P., 'Little Brother be at Peace: the Priest as Holy Man in the Nineteenth-Century Ghetto', *Studies in Church History*, xix (1982), 191-206

COPLESTONE-CROW, B., 'The Dual Nature of the Irish Colonization of Dyfed in the Dark Ages', *Studia Celtica*, xvi-xvii (1981-2), 1-24.

COUSENS, S.H., 'Settlement before the Norman Conquest', *Swansea and its Region,* ed. W.G.V. Balchin (Swansea, 1971), pp.133-45.

COWLEY, F.G., 'Religion and Education', *Swansea. An Illustrated History,* ed. Glanmor Williams (Swansea, 1990), pp. 145-76.

CRONIN, J.M.C., 'Itinerant Missionaries in Glamorgan in the Eighteenth Century', *St Peter's Magazine,* iv, no. 8 (1924), 228-33.

CRONIN, J.M.C., 'Catholicism in Swansea (1805-1808)', *St Peter's Magazine,* ix, no. 3, (1929),71-5.

CRONIN, J.M.C., 'Catholicism in Swansea (1808-29)', *St Peter's Magazine,* ix, no. 4, (1929),108-12.

DAVIES, E.T., *Religion in the Industrial Revolution in South Wales* (Cardiff, 1965).

DE BREFFNY, B., *Irish Family Names, Arms, Origins and Localities* (Dublin, 1982).

DILLON, M., 'The Irish Settlements in Wales', *Celtica,* xii (1977), 1-11.

DODD, A.H., 'Wales and Ireland from Reformation to Revolution', *Studies in Stuart Wales,* (Cardiff, 1952), pp.76-109.

FENN, R.W.D., 'Christian Origins in Glamorgan', *Glamorgan Historian,* (1963), 122-135.

FIELDER, G.D., 'Public Health and Hospital Administration in Nineteenth-Century Swansea and West Glamorgan' (Unpublished M.A. Thesis, University College of Swansea, 1962).

GRANT, R.K.J., *On the Parish* (Cardiff, 1988).

HICKEY, J.V., 'The Origin and Growth of the Irish Community in Cardiff' (Unpublished M.A. Thesis, University College, Cardiff, 1959).

HICKEY, J.V., *Urban Catholics, Urban Catholicism in England and Wales from 1829 to the Present Day* (London, 1967).

The History of the Irish in Britain. A Bibliography, ed. M. J. Hickman (London, 1980).

The Irish in the Victorian City, ed. R. Swift (London, 1985).

The Irish Sea Province in Archaeology and History, ed. D. Moore (Cardiff, 1970).

JACKSON, J.A., *The Irish in Britain* (London, 1963).

JACKSON, K.H., 'Notes on the Ogham Inscriptions of Southern Britain', *The Early Cultures of North-West Europe,* ed. C. Fox

(Cambridge, 1950), pp.199-213.

JENKINS, P., 'Connections between the Landed Communities of Munster and South Wales, c. 1660-1780', *Journal of the Cork Historical and Archaeological Society*, xi (1985), 95-101

JONES, B., *St Joseph's, Aberavon. A Parish and its People* (Aberavon, 1987).

JONES, D.J.V., 'A Dead Loss to the Community'. The Criminal Vagrant in Mid-Nineteenth-Century Wales', *Welsh History Review*, viii, no. 2 (1977), 312-43.

JONES, I.H., "Early Christian Monuments of Gower", *Gower*, x (1957), 66-74.

JONES, I.H., 'The Oldest Gower Bell', *Gower*, xi (1958), 10-12.

LEES, L.H., *Exiles of Erin. Irish Migrants in Victorian London* (Manchester, 1979).

LEWIS, C.R., 'The Irish in Cardiff in the mid-Nineteenth Century', *Cambria*, vii (1980), 13-41.

LYNE, G.J., 'Lewis Dillwyn's visit to Waterford, Cork and Tipperary in 1809' in *JCHAS*, xci, (1986), 85-104.

MACKINDER, H.J., *Britain and the British Seas* (Oxford, 1930).

MACLYSAGHT, E., *The Surnames of Ireland* (Shannon, 1969).

MASSON, U., 'The Development of the Irish and Roman Catholic Communities of Merthyr Tydfil and Dowlais in the Nineteenth Century' (Unpublished M.A. thesis, University of Keele, 1975).

MEYER, K., 'Early Relations between Gael and Brython', *THSC* (1895-6), 55-86.

NASH-WILLIAMS, V.E., *The Early Christian Monuments of Wales* (Cardiff, 1950).

NI MHUIRIOSA, M., *Gaeil agus Breatnaigh Anallód* (Dublin, 1974).

O'BRIEN, J., *Old Afan and Margam* (Aberavon, 1927).

O'BRIEN, J., *St Joseph's Church, Aberavon. The Origin and Development of the Mission* (Aberavon, 1932).

O'CATHASAIGH, T., 'The Déisi and Dyfed', *Éigse, A Journal of Irish Studies*, xx (1984), 1-33.

O'CONNOR, K., *The Irish in Britain* (London, 1972).

O'LEARY, P., 'Anti-Irish Riots in Wales, 1826-82', *Llafur*, v, no. 4, (1991-2), 27-36.

O'LEARY, P., 'Immigration and Integration. A Study of the Irish in Wales, 1798-1922' (Unpublished Ph.D. Thesis, University of Wales, 1989).

O'LEARY, P., 'Irish Immigration and the Catholic Welsh District', 1840-1850', *Politics and Society in Wales, 1840-1922*, ed. G.H. Jenkins (Cardiff, 1988).

O'MUIRITHE, D., 'The Anglo-Normans and their English Dialect of South-East Wexford', *The English Language in Ireland*, ed. D. O'Muirithe (Dublin, 1977), pp.37-55.

O'MURCHADHA, D., *Family Names of County Cork* (Dun Laoghaire, 1985).

O'RAHILLY, C. , *Ireland and Wales. Their Historical and Literary Relations* (London, 1924).

PARRY, J., 'The Tredegar Anti-Irish Riots of 1882', *Llafur*, iii, no. 4 (1983), 20-23.

PRICE, G., 'Irish in Early Britain', *The Languages of Britain* (London, 1984), pp.28-38.

PRICE, R.T., 'The Origin of the Irish Community in Greenhill, Swansea' (Unpublished thesis, Diploma in Local History, University College of Swansea, 1989).

RICHARDS, J.W., *Reminiscences of the Early Days of the Parish and Church of St Joseph's, Greenhill, Swansea* (Swansea, 1919).

RICHARDS, M., 'The Irish Settlements in South-West Wales. A Geographical Approach', *JRSAI*, xc (1960), 133-62.

RIDD, T., 'The Development of Municipal Government in Swansea in the Nineteenth Century' (Unpublished M.A. Thesis, University College of Swansea, 1955).

ROBERTS, R.O., 'The Smelting of Non-Ferrous Metals since 1750', *Glamorgan County History, v: Industrial Glamorgan from 1700-1970*, ed. A.H. John and G. Williams (Cardiff, 1980).

SPENCER, G., *Catholic Life in Swansea. The Centenary of St David's Church, Swansea, 1847-1947* (Swansea, 1947).

Sundays in Wales. Visits to the Places of Worship of the Quakers, the Unitarians, the Roman Catholics, and the Jews, by a Week-Day Preacher (Swansea, 1859).

THOMAS, C., 'Irish Colonists in South-West Britain', *World Archaeology*, v, no. 1 (1973), 5-13.

TOFT, L.A., 'The Celtic Church Monuments in Gower', *Gower,* xxxv (1984), 33-7.

WADE-EVANS, A.W., *Nennius's History of the Britons* (London, 1938).

WILLIAMS, A.M., 'Migration and Residential Patterns in Mid-Nineteenth-Century Cardiff', *Cambria*, vi, no.2 (1979), 1-27.

WILLIAMS, G., 'Religion and Belief', *The City of Swansea, Challenges and Change,* ed. R.A. Griffiths (Stroud, 1990), pp.17-33.

WOODHAM-SMITH, C., *The Great Hunger. Ireland, 1845-9* (London, 1962).